Galahad
Books
New York City

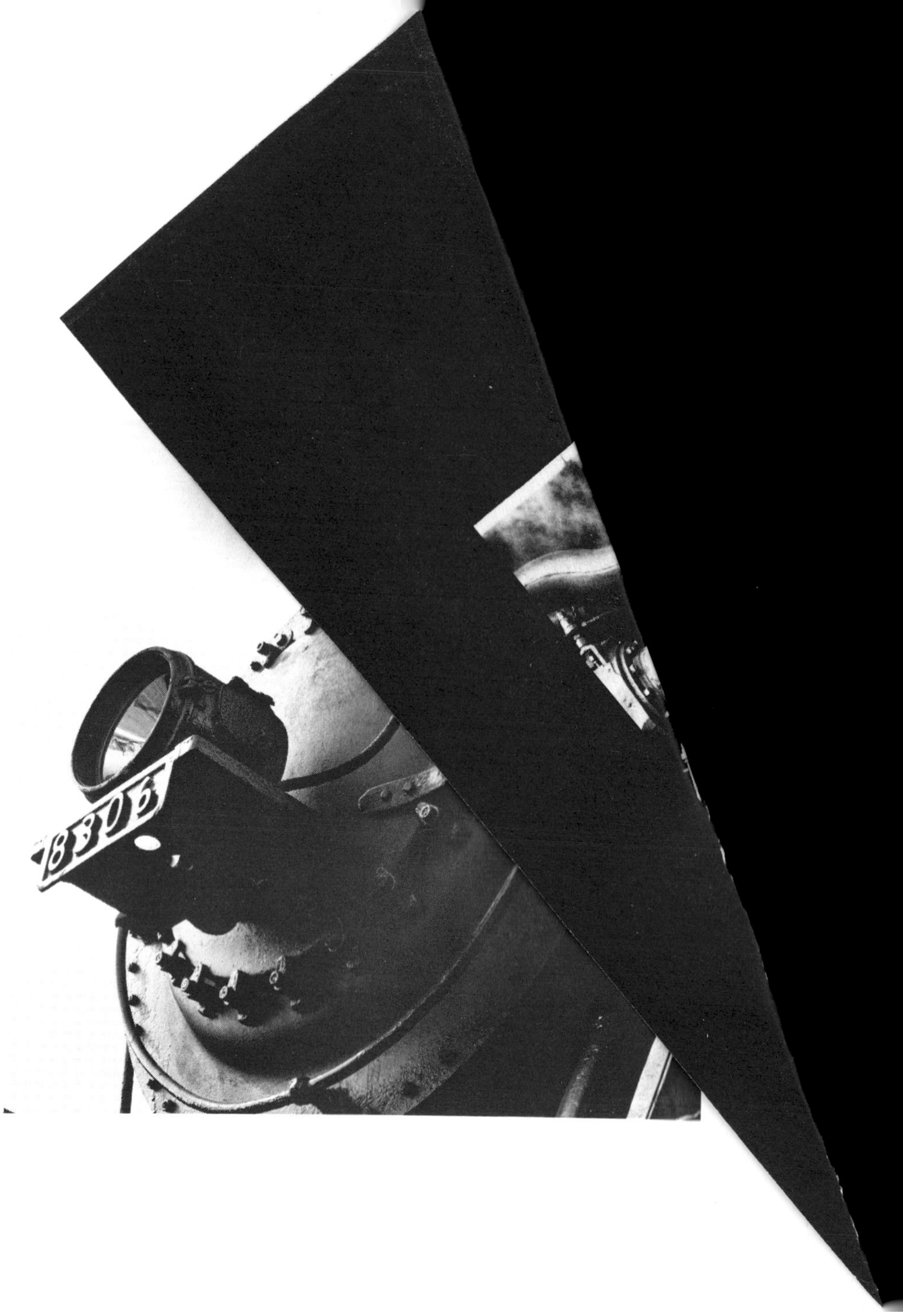

PORTRAIT OF THE RAILS

FROM STEAM TO DIESEL

by Don Ball, Jr.

introduction
by David P. Morgan

To Fenner

Standard Book Number 0-88365-100-9 Library of Congress Catalog Card Number 74-77007

Contents

Introduction by David P. Morgan

Boyhood recollection

Close of a day

1 A train is a train
page 29

2 Streamliners, streamlining and speed
page 57

3 Great steam pictorial
page 93

4 They also serve who only stand and wait...
page 167

5 Diesels–colorful couriers of change
page 201

6 Coming events cast their shadows before them
page 251

Photographic credits

Index

This book had to be. It is the end result of a boyhood-to-manhood love affair with railroads—and I am grateful for the many opportunities I have had to spend long happy hours at trackside, watching and photographing America's great trains. I am grateful, too, for the many friendships I have made along the way: the fellow rail friends, engine crews, station agents, superintendents, operators, dispatchers, "brass," and a host of others. I am especially grateful for that comraderie which exists among rail photographers everywhere—many of whom have contributed some of their finest work to PORTRAIT OF THE RAILS.

In particular, I'd like to thank David Morgan, an inspired writer who has devoted a lifetime to writing about, and bringing graphically to his readers, his own deep, personal love of railroading. Personally, I consider him a genius in his field.

Special appreciation also goes to Bob Lewis of Simmons-Boardman, and Freeman Hubbard and Gorton T. H. Wilbur of Railroad Magazine, who made statistical information available to me.

Appreciation also goes to Bob Morton, Frank DeLuca and the staff at New York Graphic Society, who have been so helpful and cooperative in giving me a "green board" with the editorial and picture content in this volume. Perhaps I've even made rail enthusiasts out of a few of them!

Finally, I'll forever be grateful to Leila Mehle, Jack Pontin, my Dad and my long-suffering wife, Linda. Without their enthusiasm this book would have been, at best, long delayed in completion.

I am everlastingly indebted to the many friends and fellow rail photographers who have contributed to this book. I regret very deeply that space does not permit inclusion of their names with each photograph. A complete list of credits, pictures and photographers will be found at the end of this book.

Don Ball, Jr.

122
326
ATLANTIC COAST

606
606
AUTOMATIC
TRAIN CONTROL
SAFETY FIRST ALWAYS

Introduction

James J. Hill, Empire Builder, builder of "the best possible line," builder of the Great Northern, said it best: "Most men who have really lived have had, in some shape, their great adventure. This railway is mine."

Those of us who instinctively find that most things which move are inherently more interesting than most things which are fixed, those of us who savored and partook of the railroad age before it was nearly eclipsed by I-System concrete and jet contrails, know whereof the old gentleman from St. Paul spoke. Burned deep in our hearts and minds is the evidence of the railway adventure: the bigger-than-life steam locomotion that was its hallmark, the endless, uncountable columns of box cars, refers and gons rolling toward the passes of Cajon, Feather River and Stampede, the Pullmans full of made-down uppers and lowers, and the men who hooped up green tissues of orders, baled coal with No. 5 scoops, wrote up waybills, and tamped ballast.

Oh Lord, but it will take some doing for America to get that adventure out of her soul!—longer to remove its meaning. Casey Jones and Commodore Vanderbilt, Altoona and Pocatello, *20th Century Limited* and *Orange Blossom Special,* Katy and Espee, Alco and Baldwin, high iron and clickety-clack. Talk about wheels! America's first wheels were steel wheels, flanged wheels: wheels that rolled us beyond the compass of sluggish rivers and sleepy steamboats, wheels that turned territories into states, wheels that made it possible for farm boys to leave when dreams brought on by a midnight whistle could no longer be denied.

Where did you first experience Jim Hill's great adventure? Tucked in between the whitest of sheets, behind green curtains swaying off a carpeted aisle, caught up in this sleeping-car vessel of steel you were riding off to camp, to college, to a war in places you couldn't pronounce? Did you encounter the railroad outside the screen door of a frame depot from which emanated the mystery of Morse code, over whose eaves hung the arms of a train order board at half mast? Did your back yard come to grips with a big

Long Island Ten-Wheeler gathering speed out of Jamaica with a half-thousand oblivious commuters caught up in folded evening newspapers behind her accelerating stack talk?

No matter. To each his own individual, private, imperishable, revered involvement with this steel adventure; hopefully, this steam and steel adventure. No need to explain; in essence, in finality, it cannot be explained, only alluded to, mentioned, cited as evidence. How to recite that first fusion of steam against pistons that lifted and lowered eight sets of main and side rods of a Norfolk & Western Mallet, taking the slack out of the couplers of a hundred and more trailing coal cars, beginning the journey of 8000 tons of bituminous to the bottom end of a smelter? It can't be done, honestly. How to recount that gray-orange flash that was the *Afternoon Hiawatha,* threatening to take Sturtevant apart at 100 per and plus, 7-foot driving wheels and 300 pounds pressure and a nerveless hand upon the throttle managing to make the impossible daily digits in the public timetable? Don't try. Be thankful that you were around when The Event occurred, make apologies to no man.

A confession is in order here. We train-watchers, we participants in Jim Hill's great adventure—we foresaw not, never thought of, made no preparations for... the diesel. We underestimated the works of General Motors. Because it never dawned on us that anything would endanger, much less eradicate, the rule of the force that had made the railroad a commercial undertaking in the first place, across the Atlantic and a century before. What had always been would always be, like the flag, the dawn, the Mississippi, the calendar. We of the rail realm knew not the sailor's wrenching shift from sail to steam, or the farmer's more compliant change from mule to tractor. What made those steel wheels roll was steam. Steam had drawn New York and Chicago to within 16 hours of each other, steam had breasted the Alleghenies and the Rockies, steam so big and so logical and so wondrous that it would last for a thousand years.

But a thousand years turned into a hundred and some.

The invader came in sheep's clothing, labeled an "oil-electric"; a little black boxy creature tucked away on waterfronts and around grain elevators where there were supposedly fire hazards or smoke ordinances. Then, in 1934, he came on properly termed "Diesel"—but in a shiny silver, wormlike attire and named *Zephyr.* Or streamliner.

Humbug. Novelty, we said. (Never mind that he didn't need round-houses, dropped no ashes and exhaled no cinders, and could run as far as rails went without breathing hard.) Blat-blat went his horn, and anything that cleared grade crossings in that manner was an affront to the gods of high iron and the spirit of Commodore Vanderbilt, and couldn't, wouldn't last.

But he did. And if the railroad was your adventure, as it was Hill's, that was a black hour, an hour for smiting one's breast, an hour for sackcloth. And not alone for us emotionally caught up in steam, but also for all the miners and boilermakers and firemen whose wages were one with lonesome midnight whistles and cindery smoke, and I-think-I-can, I-think-I-can exhaust.

Caught up in the proposition of making peace with the diesel or losing our grip on the great adventure, we signed the truce, reluctantly sought accommodation.

The invader, for all his Detroit mass production and off-the-shelf, look-alike cast, was built of sterner stuff than we had imagined. He came first in rainbow colors and steamlined mold—in royal blue for B&O, Virginia green for Southern, Omaha orange for Big G, prairie red for Great Western. He gave no external hint of the hammering V-12's and V-16's that were his internal economy, of the axle-hung electric traction motors into which he poured his crankshaft power through generator ranks. Then, having rendered his victory total, having run off a million miles and more per engine on his first go-around, the diesel came upon us in overalls—in utilitarian format. Streamlined diesels ("covered wagons" to your working railroader) were displaced by "geeps" (general-purpose units), and... and by that time we had accepted the beast and were even mourning the departure of his prototypes—Alco's lovely long-nosed PA's; all of GM's E's; shark-noses and Centipedes; and all the other celebrities known to the intimates.

But enough. This book chronicles it all: the steam that attracted us to high iron, the diesels that replaced our first love, and most enduringly, the rails that tied the whole saga together. Except by way of warning (CAUTION: TRAIN-WATCHING MAY BE HAZARDOUS TO YOUR RATIONALITY) and in caption identification, words are herein secondary, marginal, well-nigh ineffectual. In a very real sense, the photos say it all, or at least, enough.

I mean, a grease-drenched crosshead, coupling between piston rod and main rod, bathed in steam, laid against engine truck and driving wheel: that's it, brother, A-to-Z. A Santa Fe Alco PA idling in the Los Angeles Union Passenger Terminal, face-on with grilled headlight casement, war-bonnet dress, stain of Mojave and Flagstaff on her yellow and red, air horns peeking over: that's dieselization, close up. And don't miss the shot of the engineer of a Southern 2-10-2 talking it over with small-fry admirers while his fireman flicks the cinders out of a red bandana... hero worship, that—and a hero worth the worship. Or that New York Central Niagara, coupler down, elephant ears up, exhaust light, rolling down the Hudson River like sixty, for all eternity—Standard Railroading we called it.

Time now to close the typewriter. Like a railroad conductor, I've punched your ticket and pocketed it, hopefully pointed out a high spot or two on the journey ahead through this album of motion o'er rails, checked my Hamilton against yours. It's time to retire to the last plush walkover in the coach, listen in on the insistent whistle and hard-working stack up front, and doze in a world compounded of rail joints, coupled cars, steam and diesel and steel... and you'll be the better for it. Travel easy through these pages.

David P. Morgan
Editor, TRAINS Magazine

Milwaukee, Wis.

11238
FRANKLIN

Boyhood recollection

So often, I find myself drifting back into another world, a quiet world of my boyhood, one of an America I can no longer find. Every once in a while, in fact quite often, I shut out today's invading clamor and return to the fields of crickets and meadowlarks along the railroad tracks of my Kansas youth. My boyhood world seemed uninvaded somehow —one that was always there, always tranquil, always constant, and one of which I could feel I was a part. Within it, the railroad tracks provided a fascinating, captivating involvement with faraway places and distant horizons. The great trains entered and left as if on stage, storming through their roles, and departing.

For me, every train had its own distinctive character. It was the end of the war, and the potpourri of trains was splendid. The great steam locomotives, of course, constantly excited me. Each class of engine had its own special individuality—be it the sound of its chime whistle, exhaust, bell, or clanking rods. It was always easy, say, to recognize the shrill chime of a distant 9000 on the Union Pacific, or a Rock Island 4-8-4's discordant shriek whistle, but as each engine appeared on the horizon, it somehow evoked a tremendous sense of anxiety, and each one always conveyed the same urgent feelings of excitement. Down the strong, straight, well-ballasted tracks and through the ripples of heat, the massive black locomotive made its approach, its headlight a shimmering orange glow, and a trail of billowing smoke swirling above it into the sky. Then came that pulse-quickening moment when thundering steel crashed past, followed by endless orange and yellow refers, swaying and banging, their wheels pounding out a moving rhythm over the rail joints... and then the slamming of the slack as the train slowed for Lawrence. Ten minutes later, the now vanished train still made its presence felt with the distant wail of its whistle, and the haze of coal smoke settling over the corn. As always, the quiet would return, and once again meadowlarks would be heard whistling from their poles, and once more crickets chirped in the grasses only inches away.

The summer sun beat down unmercifully; it seemed to press the hot air right down to the ground. Along the tracks the white ballast reflected the heat still more—even the creosote smelled as if it would boil any moment! From the bordering fields came the fragrance of sweet clover and alfalfa. An occasional breeze rippled over the wheat fields, rustling the golden grain like the swift incoming tide of the sea. It was wonderful just to be still.

Back in the depot, it was another fascinating boyhood world, and usually a welcome relief from the hot summer sun. Here were the ever present clicking of telegraph key and sounder, the big train-arrival board, and rows and rows of brightly colored timetables—each one a beckoning call to some distant horizon. Bamboo order hoops hanging on the wall, a big Seth Thomas clock, pads of order blanks, a railroad map of the U.S., and tickets to almost anywhere. A buzzer sounded and something was "in the circuit," meaning a train was entering the block, or signal territory; then a discordant, high-noted horn signaled the arriving westbound "motor" to Marysville. The two car gas-electric train approached and stopped almost unnoticed; the conductor came into the depot for orders, and before long the peculiar conveyance was underway, burbling out of town. Some people started to assemble in the waiting room, an agent chalked up "On Time" under "Remarks" on the train-arrival board for the eastbound *Kansan*, and soon the station rapidly became a hive of activity. A mail truck drove up, joined by another from the Railway Express Agency. On the platform, the Baggage Master began positioning his wagons, and one of the agents prepared to hoop-up orders to the engine crew. Out of the west came the sound of a distant whistle.

My own favorite place to stand was way up past the station, next to the ubiquitous water plug. The *Kansan's* big two-toned gray mountain type rounded the bend, ringing its bell and trailing a combination of gray and yellow cars, half hidden in brake shoe smoke. As always, the locomotive stopped right by me and the crew would go about their business: the fireman up on the tender grabbing for the water spout with a long clanging hook, the engineer oiling around, and thoroughly checking his steed.

And what a fascinating life it was around the engine!—an ever-present multitude of sounds from escaping steam, fury of the fire, throb of panting air pumps, and harmonic buzz of the generator. Soon the engineer and fireman would be back up in the cab, behind the backhead of brass valves, gauges and controls, hosing down the deck, building up a good head of steam. The hollow sounding draw of water through the injector, grinding of the stoker screw, and roar of the blower through the big stack. Those wonderful blended smells of hot oil and grease, steam and coal smoke! The hiss from the butterfly door activator, ding and clang of the fireman's shovel and the iron clank of closing firebox doors. The safety pops raised trails of steam into the hot Kansas air, and for a moment the big machine seemed to breathe, like a sprinter waiting for the starter's gun. The highball was given and sand started to hit the rails. The rails suddenly felt the bite of the eight big drivers, the stack loudly proclaiming to the heavens, heaving up a sooty plume of smoke. Windows, filled with people, passed by me at an ever-increasing speed. The final, quick *click-click-click*, markers, a swirl of dust, and the *Kansan* was leaving town, whistling for every crossing, its staccato exhaust echoing and re-echoing off the grain elevator and nearby box cars. Down the straight track the train got smaller... the oscillating red light on the last coach danced in the Kansas heat. Soon out of sight, the *Kansan's* passing was signalled only by its distant whistle. Once again, everything seemed vacantly quiet... so quiet, in truth, that the piping call of a distant meadowlark could be heard, while sundrenched hollyhocks nodded in the sultry breeze. The rest of the day's activities would be mostly big freights, and the afternoon return of the "mixed" from Leavenworth behind its diminutive 2-8-0.

But after all is said and done, the real high point of my boyhood day was back across the Kaw River, towards evening, and along the single track main of the Santa Fe's Topeka line. At the dead end of my brick-paved street a "sitting" wall overlooked the track. No one ever seemed to be around, and I used to call it my "private wall." Sitting there I could hear the distant hum of the flour mill down the track, as well as an occasional outboard out on the river. Purple martins flittered overhead and cardinals whistled their evening songs from the phone wires. Shadows grew longer, and out in the western sky towering cumulus clouds slowly pushed upward, forming one of nature's most beautiful backdrops. Trains could still be heard across the river on the busy joint tracks of the Union Pacific and Rock Island. Never mind them; I was waiting for my favorite train.

A distant split high-to-low air horn blew for a crossing a mile east of the station—a mile and a half from my wall-side seat. I listened and waited. Ten minutes later, after a stop at the old brick station, the guttural growl of sleek diesels grew louder. That first glimpse of slant-nosed red, yellow, and silver diesels, highlighted by a patch of sunlight, completely captivated me. Six thousand steel horses roared out from under the river bridge, rounded the bend and quickly rushed past, ushering a silver-world of people to faraway places. A shiny observation car beautifully wrapped-up the sleek train, and in a brief moment it disappeared around the bend. The wonderful aroma from the dining car mixed with the diesel's breath and lingered for a few moments. Almost immediately the red semaphore lifted to yellow, and another day would have to pass before I would again see the *Kansas Cityan* in flight. It was time to go home, along the brick sidewalk, under the giant elms.

Over the years, during quiet moments, the great trains of my childhood still thunder in my memory. Thankfully, it seems as though the summer evenings on Ohio Street were only yesterday... those magic evenings that we sat out on the front porch glider waiting for darkness to slowly close in. Up and down the street, neighbors came out on their porches to welcome the coolness of evening. Cicadas buzzed high up in the great elms. I can still see the fireflies blinking, and distant heat lightning silhouetting the huge trees, as we sat out on the dark front porch. A night hawk "pi-eeked" high up over towards town and the great trains whistled on. Towards mid-evening—although nobody mentioned it—I knew we would all be listening for the *Grand Canyon* to leave town, past the end of our street and out across the dark distant fields I knew so well. The lovely whistle of its 2900 seemed to tell us that day was done. I would head for bed, but dared not fall asleep lest I might miss the *Antelope*, due to depart twenty minutes behind the *Grand Canyon*.

A boy's view of the Union Pacific through a Brownie.

Close of a day

At 1:40 PM on March 27, 1960, Grand Trunk Western's U-3b 4-8-4 6319 chuffed out of Brush Street Station in Detroit with train No. 21, bound for Durand, Michigan, 67 miles northwest. A few minutes later, a second 4-8-4, 6322, also bound for Durand, blasted the sunny skies, trudging out of Detroit with 21 cars of second No. 21.

As always, chime whistles echoed through the outlying communities of Bloomfield Hills, Highland Park, Royal Oak, Holly, and Trenton. People along the line were used to 6319 and 6322, as well as any other steamers that happened to be dispatched out of Durand and Pontiac, so this particular Sunday afternoon, March 27th, was just like any other day to most people who might have heard the 6319 and 6322.

On the same afternoon, a few hundred miles to the northeast, Canadian Pacific's P-1 class 2-8-2, 5107, sounded her whistle west of town, and pulled into Brownville Jct., Maine, with train No. 518 from Megantic, Quebec, 117 miles away. Chances are the citizens along the way had heard 5107's high-pitched chime whistle echoing through the hills, as they had so many times before.

The next day, Trains No. 21 and No. 518 ran as always—but the muttering drone of internal combustion diesel engines, and bleating air horns were very much in evidence. What had started one hundred and twenty-nine years earlier, when the steam locomotive, "Best Friend of Charlestown," hauled the first steam train in regular service, now had come to an end. During the preceding incredibly short span of ten years, the fires had been dropped, one by one, from the steamers on virtually every class I railroad in America.

Many of us feel that March 27, 1960, marked the end of America's most romantic and glorious era. (Rumors persist over the years that the Norfolk and Western occasionally assigned one of their remaining Y-6's to a mine run out of Williamson, W. Va., through May of 1960. Records are not available for documentation, but it would be only fitting that the Norfolk and Western have the distinction of operating the last steam locomotive in class I revenue service).

For me it was the end of a most meaningful part of my life: a thousand-and-one experiences, now all partially jelled, for which I'll be forever grateful. Yes, the rails that gave me an intimate acquaintance with this great country are still there, in most places, but without steam something is really missing—and it's much more than just boyhood wonder. The late Lucius Beebe once said, "It is no accident of circumstance that the most beautiful devisings and artifacts in the American record have all been associated with motion and movement, the transport of things and people all going somewhere else." When we had steam, we witnessed its wonderful motion and heard its every movement, and as we watched, we knew it wasn't easy to get to that "somewhere else." We remained a captive audience while the great trains came and went. With the jet plane and superhighway, of course, this has all changed.

It may be easier to see this country now, but it is not the same. We occasionally cross over a railroad track, and leave it en route to wherever we're going; but, oh, how I would love to return to a quiet countryside where, once again, it would be a steam locomotive that came and went—leaving an indelible impression on my mind and soul.

This book is not about the end of steam, nor is it a journey to the backwaters, away from the thundering surf. It is a close-up look at the great and wonderful trains which captured America's fancy during our most colorful industrial revolution; a deep-toned tribute to a vanished American past.

Selfishly, this book is something almost exclusively and essentially personal; but it's also something I want very much to share. A good deal of my own photography is missing; this is intentional, for too many personal experiences portrayed by one individual could easily detach the reader from his own personal involvement. The great photographers represented here join with me in a deep and abiding common interest and purpose, and to them I shall always be grateful.

A train is a train

1

The sole purpose of this book is to portray vividly what I believe to have been America's most colorful industrial transition: the gradual change in the railroad industry from its shaky, post-depression days of recovery to the imaginative innovations in equipment which helped restore sorely needed traffic prior to the build-up of our war economy in the 1940's.

The introduction of air-conditioning and high-speed travel were the prime factors in bringing the public's attention back to the railroads. The fascinating debate continued on the developing diesel engine and its possible future application as a prime mover of passengers and freight. It would quickly be settled, changing the industry more than all other developments in railroading during the preceding 100 years.

In mid-1934, which I consider to be the start of the railroad industry's turn around, the most prevalent type of locomotive was the 2-8-0 Consolidation, of which 11,266 were in service—roughly 47% of all locomotives on the nation's rails. Their average age was almost 26 years, and the repair costs alone were enough to dictate a need for newer power. Management and operating personnel were well aware of this bleak picture, as well as the fact that the nation's production and commerce was less than 60% of what it had been from 1925 through 1929. The government, through its Public Works Administration, authorized loans to the railroads with the understanding that the monies would go into new equipment and supplies. Production, employment and service were all to benefit.

Great changes were in store for the railroads, and a new spirit of adaptability to change—both physical and psychological—was very much needed. In short, the industry's thinking and policies had to be totally reoriented to the tasks of meeting competition and greatly increasing its volume of business. Initially this meant vast improvements in service, utilizing, in most cases, the equipment it already had.

Few railroads enjoyed as much fan following and employee allegiance as the New Haven, yet few railroads were photographed less. The late Kent Cochrane spent a good portion of his life stalking the rails of the New Haven, a line he held almost in reverence. Kent was a superb, dedicated lensman—as evidenced by the photograph at left of the splendid passing of New Haven's symbol freight AO-1 from Hartford to Maybrook on the Waterbury line. The pipe-laden class L-1 2-10-2s were standard power on this section of the railroad.

In 1925, a new locomotive design was introduced by Lima and the dawn of Super-Power steam locomotives had begun. Lima's new engine, a 2-8-4, utilized an enormous firebox whose evaporating surfaces exceeded those of all other locomotives and required a two-axled trailing truck for support. The Boston & Albany put the first demonstrator to the test on its rugged Berkshire profile and promptly placed an order for fifty-five of the power-packed 2-8-4s! These, and all future 2-8-4s, were dubbed "Berkshire types." The muscular 1422 hurries a caboose through Weston Park Siding, Mass.

One of the finest action shots ever taken is of B&A's train No. 13, *The Wolverine* hitting an easy 80 on the Weston Park curve shortly after the 1422 powered caboose hop cleared the main through Riverside. B&A engineer-photographer, H. W. Pontin, certainly picked the right spot for these two. The Hudson was also Lima built, using the plans of parent New York Central.

New York Central's L2-c Mohawk No.2890 storms out of the westbound bore of Breakneck tunnel with 100-plus cars. Those 69-inch drivers will have no trouble maintaining speed on the "Water Level Route." This L2-c is equipped with footboards, usually scorned by rail photographers, but essential for brakemen when working in yards.

Across the Hudson, on the Central's West Shore Line, New York, Ontario and Western's sole Y-1 Mountain No. 402 rolls splendidly down the 4-track main with home-bound weekenders from the Catskills. Alas, in 1951, ten years after this photograph was made, the O&W occupied but one page in The Official Guide; now, the railroad is all but a memory, having ceased operations on March 29, 1957.

In an amphitheater-like setting *(right)*, one of the 574 Pennsy class L-1s Mikados does what she knows how to do best—lug a heavy train up a steep grade. With no stoker, this handbomber most likely requires two strong backs to keep a good head of steam up on the long grade out of Marysville. The tank car on 8197's drawbar has been converted to an auxilary water tank to do away with any hill-climbing water stops that might stall the train.

One notable exception to these "pre-diesel days" shots is Bud Rothaar's stunningly dramatic action of Pennsy's M1-b No.6117, westbound, steaming down the 4-track boulevard towards Duncannon, and an "approach-medium" on the board. This was railroading for all eternity.

8197

2490
2490

As much a part of the sentimental southern tradition as moonlight, magnolias and mockingbirds was the sight of well-groomed, classic-lined locomotives headending a colorful array of trains. Certainly the Seaboard 2-10-2, seen above at the left swinging over the Southern Railway's main at Weems, Ala., displays a symetrically turned boiler that exemplifies the finest in clean-lined simplicity. Above, No.818 on a bread-and-butter run so typical of railroading in the Deep South scurries along the Seaboard's iron near Floyd, Georgia; while below at left, a Southern 2-8-2 works a Birmingham local up a long pine-bordered stretch of single track. To the right, loblolly pines get a liberal dusting of coal smoke from Southern's lumbering simple expansion 2-8-8-2 No.4056 as she works half a mile of high cars under the Seaboard at Weems. This Ls-2 class articulated was Southern's largest and most powerful steam locomotive.

The Southern Railway was noteworthy for its scrupulously maintained, beautifully painted steam power. Two classic beauties were the Virginia green and gold-trimmed Ps-4 class 4-6-2s and Ts-1 class 4-8-2s. Resplendent green and gold 6497 whips out of a tunnel, across the Cumberland River and into a beautiful springtime at Burnside, Kentucky, with the popular Miami-bound *Royal Palm.* The 6497, which has powered the train from Cincinnati, will run as far as Macon, Geo., where two light-weight Pacifics will take over on the lighter cinder-ballasted rail to Jacksonville.

Southern's class Ks Consolidation No.837 arrives in East St. Louis, Ill., just ahead of the setting sun. This gleaming bell-clanging 2-8-0, painted in gloss black with gold numerals probably dazzled photographer Bill Barham. Few railroads would have bestowed such loving care and attention upon a 2-8-0; but on Southern, this was recognition due a faithful little servant.

PENNSYLVANIA
5498

NEW YORK CENTRAL
5248

No two steam locomotives were more famed, acclaimed, photographed and modeled than the legendary K-4 of the Pennsylvania and the classic Hudson of the New York Central. During the opulent years of railroad travel, the K-4 powered the *Broadway Limited,* and the Hudson powered *The 20th Century Limited.* Both trains were grand conveyances that only such rivals as the Pennsy and Central would lavish upon their patrons. The competition was keen, centering on elegance, speed and service.

Above, the *Golden Arrow* makes a picturesque departure out of Chicago after slamming across the 21st Street Bridge. The 80-inch drivered K-4 (the "bowstring" for the *Arrow*) is already approaching full stride.

One of Chicago & North Western's class E Pacifics *(above)* gets a good roll on a Geneva, Ill. bound local. The sprightly 1909 vintage 4-6-2 is fresh from the shops and the boys should be proud of her. Oh yes, that's one of those oil-electric engines over on the side track.

Chicago's fascinating maze of trackwork has always provided the rail photographer with an ample variety of locations. Vernon Seaver caught the dramatic departures of Erie's *Midlander* behind a regal K-5 Pacific *(above right)* and Chicago & Eastern Illinois' *The Dixieland* behind a Pacific especially assigned to this train. There's nothing like a crisp wintry day for capturing the drama of steam and these shots provide powerful testimonials.

2934

Burlington's O-la 2-8-2 No.4945 *(below)* has just received class three repairs in the West Burlington, Iowa shops and is charging east through Downer's Grove, Illinois, with a vengeance. The usual practice with most operating departments was to assign freshly overhauled power to less exacting runs. The "Q" obviously was caught short and 4945 with a mile of cars is a sight to behold!

The Chicago & Alton Railroad, over whose rails many of George Pullman's first steel cars rode, provided colorful competition on the Chicago to St. Louis run and offered its patrons luxuries usually found only on the more prestigious name trains. High stepping Pacific No.5298 *(below, at right)* bounds down the well manicured main with the premier *Alton Limited*, resplendent in Tuscan red and maroon livery. The spring meadows and field flowers complete this three-quarter vignette of railroading in the grand manner.

On the following pages two well-proportioned Missouri Pacific "hogs" muscle freight up grade through the lush surroundings of Kirkwood, Mo. The 64-inch drivered 2-10-2's exhaust is quick; while the 75-inch drivered 4-8-4 road engine's laboring voice is slower. Both fires are clean and the stack talk is magnificent! For the unacquainted, that helper on the point is a former Wabash L-1 of 1917 vintage, and the road engine was originally a 63-inch drivered 2-8-4 rebuilt at the MoP's Sedalia shops.

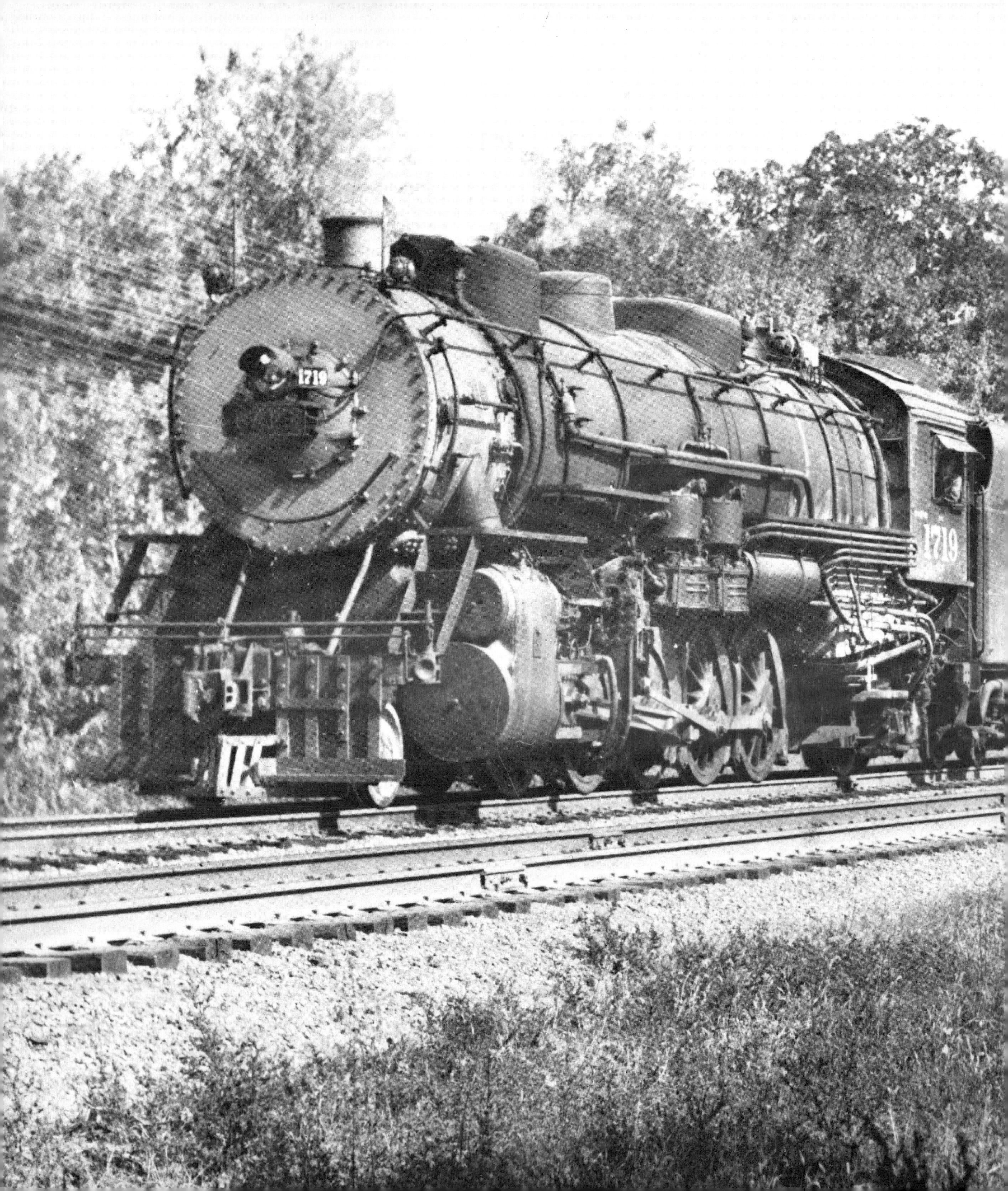
1719
1719

2119
1719

1555

MILGRAM
4058

Missouri Pacific's magnificently proportioned 2-8-2 No.1555 *(above left)* steps quickly with a California perishable block. Even in its passenger timetables, the road advertised its fast California freight connections, and this "Mike" certainly proves the point.

Neighboring Rock Island leaned heavily on sixty-two 4-8-2s to perform similar chores on merchandise as well as on heavy passenger runs. One of their class M-50a 4-8-2s *(below left)* backs through Kansas City's Union Station, its ownership proudly emblazoned on its tender.

Like the Missouri Pacific and Rock Island, the Rio Grande also had handsome steam power that displayed a purposeful appearance. No exceptions were Rio Grande's 14 class M-64 Northerns built in 1929 by Baldwin and capable of handling the heavy trains from Denver to Salt Lake City, 745 torturous miles. Above, 4-8-4 No. 1702 powers the *Exposition Flyer* up South Boulder Canyon's 2% grade at a steady 25 miles an hour.

The Union Pacific's 4-12-2 was a marvelous marriage of machinery and was always my personal favorite. The sight of one of these 3-cylinder behemoths banging away in multiple shouts—each exhaust seemingly trying to beat the other out the stack—will forever live in my memory. The first of this great breed *(above)* was photographed 20 miles west of Sherman Hill, Wyo. on May 13, 1933.

In 1927, the Denver & Rio Grande Western ordered ten huge 2-8-8-2 type single-expansion articulated locomotives to overcome the demanding three percent grade up Tennessee Pass and its 10,221 foot summit. These mammoth engines weighed over a million pounds and were the world's most powerful locomotives when built. In one of his most moving portraits of steam, Dick Kindig caught Rio Grande's 2-8-8-2 No. 3604 and 4-8-4 No. 1803 on *The Scenic Limited*, battling up the Pass near Mitchell, Colo., their thundering exhausts etching a pattern of steam against the cold Colorado sky.

At year's end 1934, two types of steam freight power presided over the nation's rails: the 2-8-2, of which there were 9,830, and the 2-10-2, of which there were 2,054. Both types had small drivers and were essentially low-speed drag engines. The Colorado & Southern stayed with a good thing and relied upon a well-maintained stable of 2-8-2s and 2-10-2s to tame the road's "up-and-down" profile. In the photograph, taken on June 26, 1938, C&S's brawny 2-10-2 No.907 works Denver-bound freight out of Trinidad, Colo. *(preceding pages)*.

3604

Below, Bill Barham caught this handsome pair of Sweeney-stacked Harriman locomotives on the eastbound *Los Angeles Limited,* thundering up the Cajon. Depending on traffic demand and fuel supply, the big boilered 2-8-2 helper will cut off at Summit, or continue on east to Barstow with the 4-8-2 road engine. The awesome, desolate beauty of Cajon Pass has lured legions of great train photographers whose names are as legendary as the locomotives themselves.

At left, two of Santa Fe's rugged 2-10-2s head down a long tangent track in a majestic Mojave setting—a backlit study of Western railroading in a land of distant horizons.

Streamliners, streamlining and speed

2

On April 16, 1934, Mr. R. Tom Sawyer of the American Locomotive Company presented an outline on diesel motive power to the Western Railway Club in Chicago. Other builders of diesels had representatives present and each voiced confidence in the future of the diesel, even its possible adaptability to passenger and freight service. There were already nearly 1000 gasoline rail cars on the nation's rails, and more important, over 100 diesel locomotives in switching and transfer service. Later in the meeting, Mr. W. L. Garrison, Assistant Manager, Locomotive Department, Ingersoll-Rand Company, pointed with pride to the fact that these 100 diesels had continued to operate in switching, transfer and branch-line service. The reliability of the oil engine was documented in prepared remarks on operating conditions, such as 20-24 hour continuous running capability at almost constant acceleration and deceleration. When the meeting broke up some hours later, one wondered how, and at what point in railroad operations would the diesel concede defeat to the steam locomotive—if at all!

Forty days after the Railway Club meeting, a sleek diesel-propelled articulated train called *Zephyr* sprinted non-stop from Denver's Union Station to Halsted Street, Chicago, in 13 hours and 5 minutes—at an average speed of 77.5 miles per hour. It made history! It was estimated that over half a million people watched the silver train's passing in the 164 cities and towns along the way. Chaucer's word for Spring wind took on a railroading connotation, and the new word D-I-E-S-E-L made an indelible impact on the American public. Speed and Diesel became synonymous.

On July 20, a standard Milwaukee F-7 Hudson steam locomotive, pulling conventional equipment, blasted out of Chicago and arrived in Milwaukee 67 minutes and 37 seconds later, averaging 75.5 miles per hour. Its top speed of 103.5 m.p.h. was sustained for over 14 miles—and this without the extraordinary precautions which had been taken for the special run of the *Zephyr*. Shortly thereafter, the Milwaukee's management announced that it had ordered new streamlined steam locomotives for the run. Speed and streamlining became synonymous with passenger (steam and diesel) railroad travel. The spirited comeback of passenger trains had begun, and throughout the next decade a colorful assortment of trains would take over this nation's rails and capture the public's fancy. Even the most popular child's book "Engine Engine No. 9" would feature a new streamlined steam engine closely resembling a Loewy-styled Pennsy K-4.

4837

After the *Zephyr,* Union Pacific launched its new M-10001 *Streamline* on a Los Angeles to New York transcontinental dash: 3,258 miles in 56 hours and 55 minutes—almost a day's time less than LA to Chicago schedules. Like *Zephyr,* the M-10001 was a lightweight self-propelled, permanently coupled train and, therefore, too inflexible for normal train operations. Steam would continue to power conventional trains. But diesel designers did not waver. In 1935, EMC, St. Louis Car, GE and Winton Engine Corporation began marketing diesels for conventional trains. The first multiple-unit diesel was Santa Fe's 1 and 1-A shown *(opposite left)* on its record-breaking run from Los Angeles to Chicago, hauling a 720 ton conventional train. Below is the first true cab diesel, also built by EMC and St. Louis Car, and powered by the Winton 201-A 900 h.p. engine. This unit was built in August, 1935 for B&O and was later sent to affiliate Alton where she was given a shovel nose. She's shown at speed on the *Abraham Lincoln,* south of Bloomington, Illinois in 1937.

Shown above is New Haven's revolutionary streamlined *Comet,* designed and built by the Goodyear-Zeppelin Corporation. This sleek train had power plants at each end, and entered service between Providence and Boston, covering the 44 miles in 44 minutes, including two stops. The *Comet* is shown on high speed tangent track near Foxboro, Mass., shortly after its June 5, 1935, inaugural.

Swinging around a rockcut is the ACF built *Rebel,* the first streamlined train in the south. Unlike the *Zephyr,* the train was not articulated (permanently coupled), nor did it sprint long distances. Between Jackson, Miss. and New Orleans, the little *Rebel* made almost 50 stops!

The Burlington placed the first high-speed diesel train into revenue service between Lincoln, Omaha and Kansas City on November 11, 1934. This train, called *Pioneer Zephyr,* was the original *Zephyr* that caught the public's fancy. The tremendous success of this train prompted Burlington to place two twelve-car *Denver Zephyrs* into service in 1936. The "Silver Knight" and "Silver Queen" head up one of the gleaming new trains at Denver's Union Station.

Not long after the photo on the left was taken a mishap occurred that management, understandably, tried to conceal. No. 1, the *Denver Zephyr*, is caught being towed into Denver by the old reliable on September 24, 1938. As with any new machine, things can go wrong; as for diesel 9907, its water pump went out, leaving it stuck with 200 h.p. and eleven cars—a moment to warm the heart of any traditional railroader.

NEW YORK
CENTRAL
LINES

On November 24, 1934, F. E. Williamson, President of the New York Central, took the wraps off the first streamlined steam locomotive, the "Commodore Vanderbilt," named for the founder of the railroad. The locomotive's "bathtub" metal covering was finished in a gun-metal lacquer with white striping. Williamson introduced the streamlined engine as evidence of the Central's belief that, despite recent developments in the use of other fuels, the day of the steam locomotive was far from past. Many statistics on decreased wind resistance, fuel savings and speed were widely flaunted and Mr. Williamson pointed to the fact that steam would continue to offer the "maximum of travel safety and comfort and speeds as high as most persons would care to travel."

Union Pacific placed its faith in a fleet of new diesel streamliners such as shown top to bottom: M-10001, the *City of Portland,* which began service on June 6, 1935, pictured leaving Cheyenne on October 28, 1938; the 1936-built *City of Denver* headed by joint-C&NW/U.P. units CD-07-A, 07-B and 07-C at Sand Creek, Colorado on September 14, 1940; and the elegant trio of 1937-built E-2s LA-1, 2 and 3 heading train No.111, the *City of Denver* into the Union Station on November 27, 1937. The last year of customized diesel building was 1937 and the era could not have ended with a more glamorous train than the 5400 h.p. *City of Los Angeles.*

On the following pages, the two competitors of a new era—the shovel-nosed *Denver Zephyr* and the grill-nosed *City of Denver* stand ready at Denver's Union Station.

DENVER ZEPHYR
SILVER KNIGHT

URLINGTON
SILVER PRINCESS

One by one, the new locomotives and trains were finding their way onto the front pages of newspapers and into the vocabulary of the general public. Talk of 100 m.p.h. travel was becoming commonplace.

A most extensive public relations campaign proclaimed the arrival, on April 30, 1935, of the Milwaukee's new streamlined A class *Hiawatha*—the first all-new streamlined steam locomotive to be constructed. No.1 is shown leaving the erecting bay at Alco's Schenectady, N.Y. shops, less than a month before entering regular 100 m.p.h. service.

Below, Baltimore & Ohio's distinctive class V-2 Hudson named "Lord Baltimore" and designed for the lightweight *Royal Blue* makes fast time on the Alton's *Abraham Lincoln.* Diesel influence is evident in the retractable coupler and strident air horn, but the hooked-up train is a lovely sight.

After moving east, I became briefly acquainted with the handsome "Shore Liners" of the New Haven. R. L. Pearson, V.P. of the railroad, accepted the first I-5 4-6-4 from Robert S. Binkerd, V.P. of Baldwin Locomotive Works, describing it as "the first fully streamlined locomotive on an Eastern railroad." Binkerd closed the ceremony stating, "if you don't get 125,000 miles or more per year out of her, we'll be back in New Haven with a search warrant." Needless to say, they did not come back! At the right, the brand new 1400 gets some grime on her skirt on a break-in run along the shoreline.

THE MILWAUKEE ROAD

Two 84-inch drivered classics were Chicago and Northwestern's olive green E-4 and Milwaukee's orange, silver and maroon F-7. At the top, Northwestern's 4008 makes child's play of the 18-car *Pacific Limited* near Dekalb, Ill. on a quick Chicago-Omaha-Chicago turn-around; below, brilliant Otto Kuhler-styled Hudson No.100 gets a roll on the elegant *Morning Hi* out of Chicago on a dreary day. Soon she'll be limbering up at 100 m.p.h.

New York Central's own efforts to streamline steam locomotives usually resulted in the "upside down bathtub" look. Central's two K-5 Pacifics 4915 and 4917, intended for the new Chicago to Detroit and Detroit to Cleveland streamlined *Mercury* assignments, were worthy of this distinction. At the right is a company publicity shot of the 4915, later spruced up for the *James Whitcomb Riley;* below, the 4917 is working an open throttle on the *Mercury.*

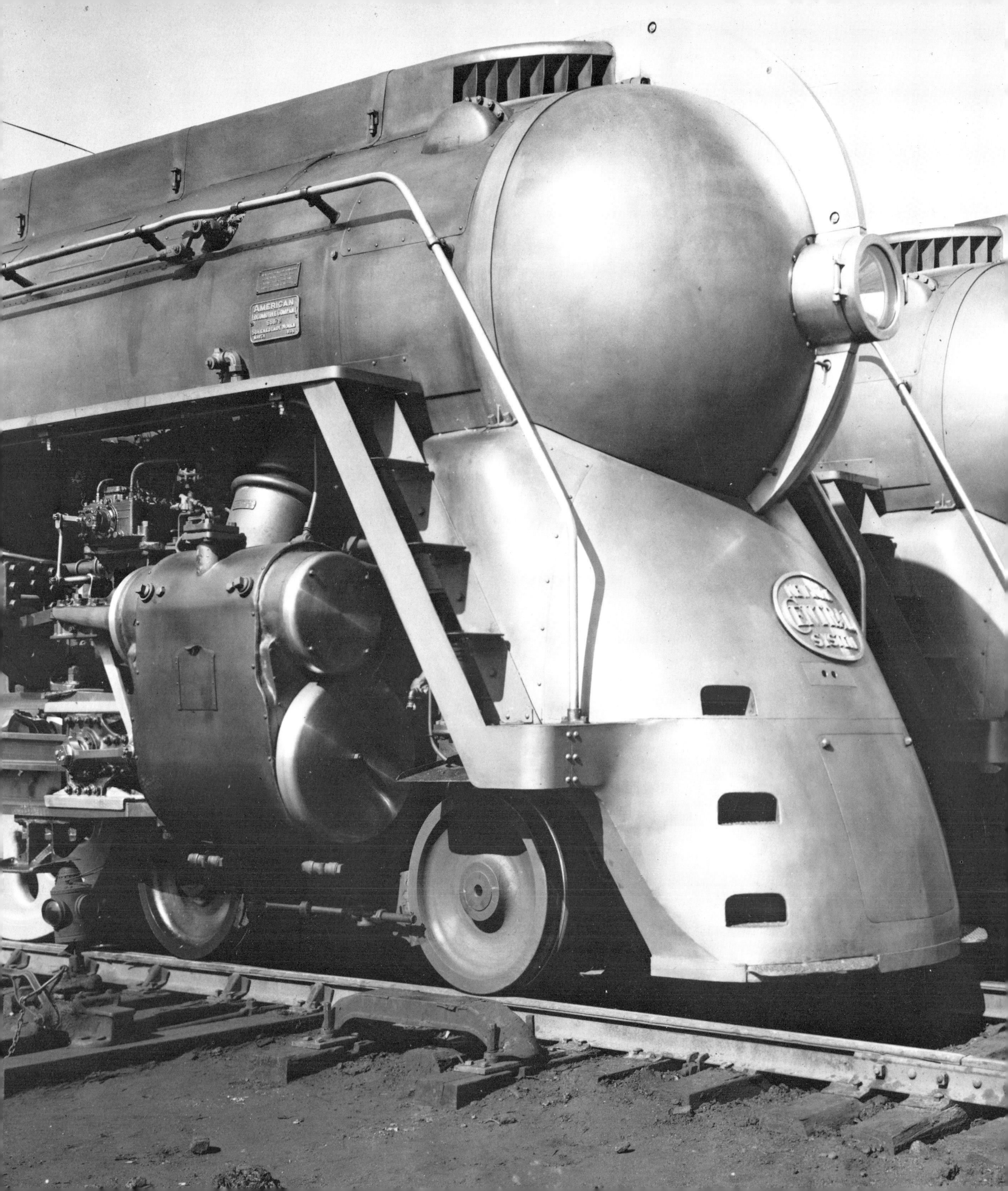
AMERICAN
LOCOMOTIVE COMPANY
NEW YORK
CENTRAL
SYSTEM

The quintessence of elegance: on the road that made money with passengers, nothing was too good for them. The New York Central featured the most streamlined steam locomotives, and the consensus was that the most beautiful locomotives of the streamlined era were the ten 1938 Dreyfuss-styled J-3 Hudsons for the *Twentieth Century Limited.* These locomotives soon became the advertised trademark of the Central at the time that the *Century* was being billed as "more than the world's newest train, but a new mode of transportation." Nos.5445, 5449 and 5451 are carefully posed for their portraits.

With or without the distinctive cowlings, the New York Central's Hudsons were considered the most handsome, best-proportioned steam locomotives ever built. *(Below left)* The crosshead, eccentric rod, side rod, main rod and Baker valve gear sparkle on this magnificent machine. At the right, this "most beautiful train in the world" departs from Chicago's La Salle Street Station with the Board of Trade building and skyline in the background.

NEW YORK
CENTRAL
SYSTEM

5928

In 1929, The Montreal Locomotive Works constructed twenty class T-1A 2-10-4s for both freight and passenger service. So successful were these giants of the Dominion that an additional ten were built in 1938, with increased boiler pressure and streamlining at the front end. These great engines were capable of handling 1,025 tons up the Canadian Rockies' 2.2% grades without assistance—an equivalent to 12,000 tons on level track. Most of their lives were spent between Calgary, Alberta and Revelstake, British Columbia, "on the hill" as C.P. men affectionately called it. O. Winston Link caught the 5928 close to full stroke beneath the lofty ramparts of the Selkirk Range.

Above right, EMD's first off-the-shelf diesel, no.51, rolls down the iron north of Philadelphia. This 3600 h.p. A-B tandem was assigned to the all-Pullman *Capitol Limited* to keep ahead of Pennsy's refurbished, steam-powered *Liberty Limited.* Today, the 51 is preserved at the B & O Museum in Baltimore. Below is Grand Trunk's frosty departure of the *Maple Leaf* out of Chicago behind one of the streamlined locomotives developed from exhaustive wind tunnel tests at the National Research Council at Ottawa. The U-4-B streamlined 4-8-4 was identical to parent Canadian National's U-4-A, the first streamlined locomotive in Canada.

Before the Pennsy finally tossed in the towel on steam production, their mechanical engineers at Altoona had one final glorious fling at high speed, high horsepower—albeit unorthodox—steam. Their S-1 class Duplex 6-4-4-6 turned out to be the largest steam passenger locomotive ever built, and one of the railroads biggest headaches on the road. The pretentious Raymond Loewy showpiece will best be remembered on exhibition at the New York World's Fair of 1939-1940 appropriately lettered "AMERICAN RAILROADS."

Near right, New York Central's No.5344, alias "Commodore Vanderbilt", returns to I.C. station Chicago in a new 1939 Dreyfuss jacket to handle the Detroit-bound *Mercury*. Admirers include the fireman, who is getting his first close look. A model of this locomotive—unstreamlined—later became the most popular item for Lionel and American Flyer. At the far right, Lehigh Valley's K-5 Pacific No.2102 struts proudly down the main in her Cornell red jacket, white pin striping and black undergear. She's 23 years old, but with the new coat and matching train, the "Valley" has entered the era of streamlining.

2102

The most powerful 4-8-4s and the last U.S. streamlined steam locomotives to operate were Norfolk & Western's Js. Designed to maintain a steady 50 m.p.h. with any passenger train on the system's severe grades and curves, these locomotives could run at the century mark when track conditions allowed. By 1958, the sleek Northerns were bumped off varnish and disgracefully downgraded to local freights. Here, the 612 rolls empty wood pulp racks towards Appomattox, Va. under an untypical dirty fire. The road foreman obviously wanted to go along for the ride!

On December 1, 1942, Mrs. Herbert H. Lehman, wife of New York's Governor, christened the new Budd-built *Empire State Express* with a bottle of New York State wine. The ceremony was broadcast coast-to-coast on CBS and the train was described as "the most comfortable and beautiful day train so far built." The new train, carrying 45,000 special mail cachets, sweeps through Garrison, N.Y. on her first run. *(Right)* In later years Dick Cook photographed the nine-car *Empire State Express* steaming grandly through Euclid, Ohio behind the Dreyfuss-designed Hudson No.5447.

NEW YORK
CENTRAL
SYSTEM

4435
2
3

Perhaps the most spectacular group of streamlined locomotives in America were the brilliant orange, red, silver and black class GS-4 "Daylights" built by Lima for the Southern Pacific in 1941.

Away from her customary role hauling the *Daylight,* No.4435 looms out of the morning mist and arrives in Los Angeles with train 1-70. The backing steamer to the right is returning to the Alhambra roundhouse. Below, another beauty is Burlington's stainless-steel paneled E-5 "Silver Speed" leaving Chicago on the head end of the *Exposition Flyer* in 1941. These diesels were production models, but for a railroad which pioneered diesels, the distinctive side trim was almost mandatory.

99

Stan Kistler made this magnificent shot of Southern Pacific's Northbound *Daylight* climbing out of Los Angeles near Chatsworth, Cal. To many train fanciers, the *Daylights* were the most beautiful trains in the world.

One of the most cleanly designed locomotives was Canadian National's big K-5a class Hudson. It was built by the Montreal Locomotive Works in 1930, with a small amount of sheet metal trim added in later years. Here, the original of the class clatters through the Bayview cross-over, enroute to Montreal with a morning train from Toronto. The flanged stack became a trademark for Canadian National 4-6-4s and 4-8-2s.

At the right, Harley Kelso has caught the original GS-4 "Daylight" waiting for the board at the east end of the Taylor yards. The Dayton Avenue Tower just beyond the signal bridge controls the busy interlocking for the roundhouse leads, yard tracks and both the Los Angeles Division (coast line) and San Joaquin Division mains.

SOUTHERN PACIFIC
4430
POLLY

In my opinion, the most handsome streamlined steam locomotives were four re-built 1927 President class Pacifics for Baltimore and Ohio's new 1946 *"Cincinnatian."* These royal blue, black and silver-trimmed pacers cut the time between Cincinnati and D.C. to eleven and a half hours. The train's seating capacity was 244, but no more than 176 seats were ever sold in order to give everyone ample room throughout the plush train. Non-fogging windows, radios, and inter-communicating telephones were introduced, and the 100 m.p.h. locomotives were fitted with special deep-chambered whistles to enable people along the way to identify the *Cincinnatian.* In this late afternoon picture, the 5302 climbs Cranberry Grade near Amblersburg, W. Va., its lovely contours highlighted.

An early user of the 4-8-4 was the Nashville, Chattanooga & St. Louis whose management recognized its dual freight and passenger capabilities. Trim 1943-built J-3 No.587 lifts the celebrated *Dixie Limited* out of Smyrna, Ga. A capped stack was required of builder Alco to preserve the "traditional hallmark" for which the road's earlier steam power was known.

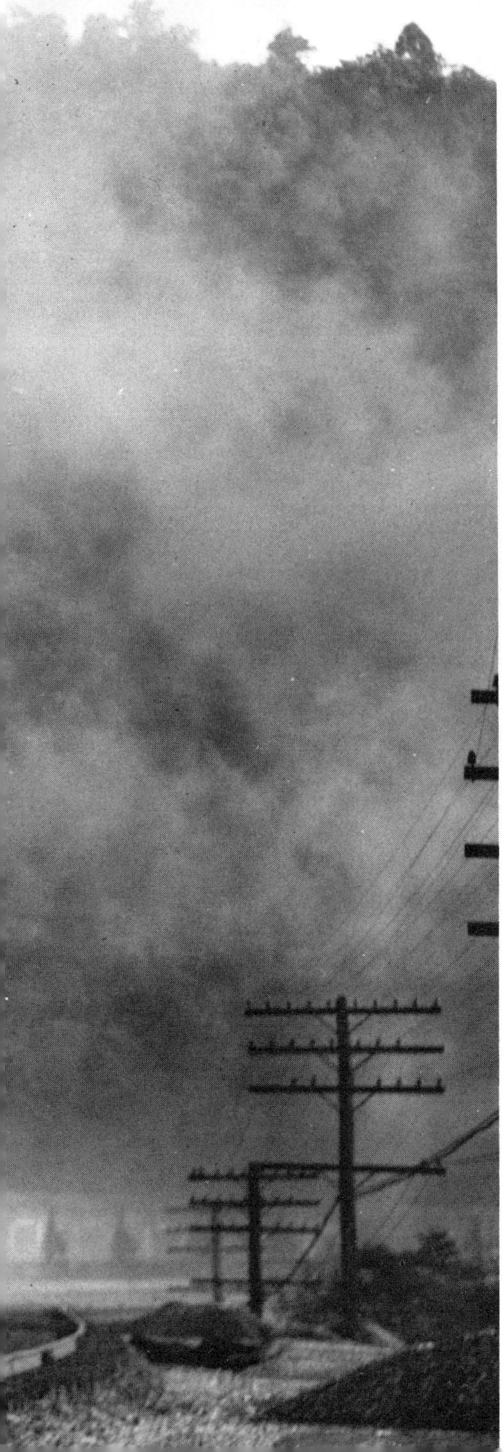

702
WABASH
702
702

900
900
TEXAS & PACIFIC

Between 1943 and 1947, Wabash rounded up seven of its older 2-8-2s and rebuilt them into virtually new 4-6-4s for the *Bluebird, Banner Blue* and *The Wabash Cannon Ball.* These blue, white and red enamel-trimmed couriers made good use of their 80-inch drivers across the flatlands, and were a stunning example of what a little imagination, engineering and paint could do.

Being a traditionalist, I detest seeing standard steam locomotives "dolled-up" with gaudy paint. I must admit, however, that a sense of splendor radiates from this beautifully proportioned 4-8-2, dashingly be-decked in blue and silver livery for Texas & Pacific's *Sunshine Special.*

The last vestige of "streamlining" was accomplished with a minimum amount of sheet metal and pipe-concealing boiler jacketing. One of the most camera-shy locomotives, and a fine example of simplified lines, was Toledo, Peoria and Western's H-10 class 4-8-4. Here, No.81 has just been cut off the *Effner Redball* to be readied for its next assignment west.

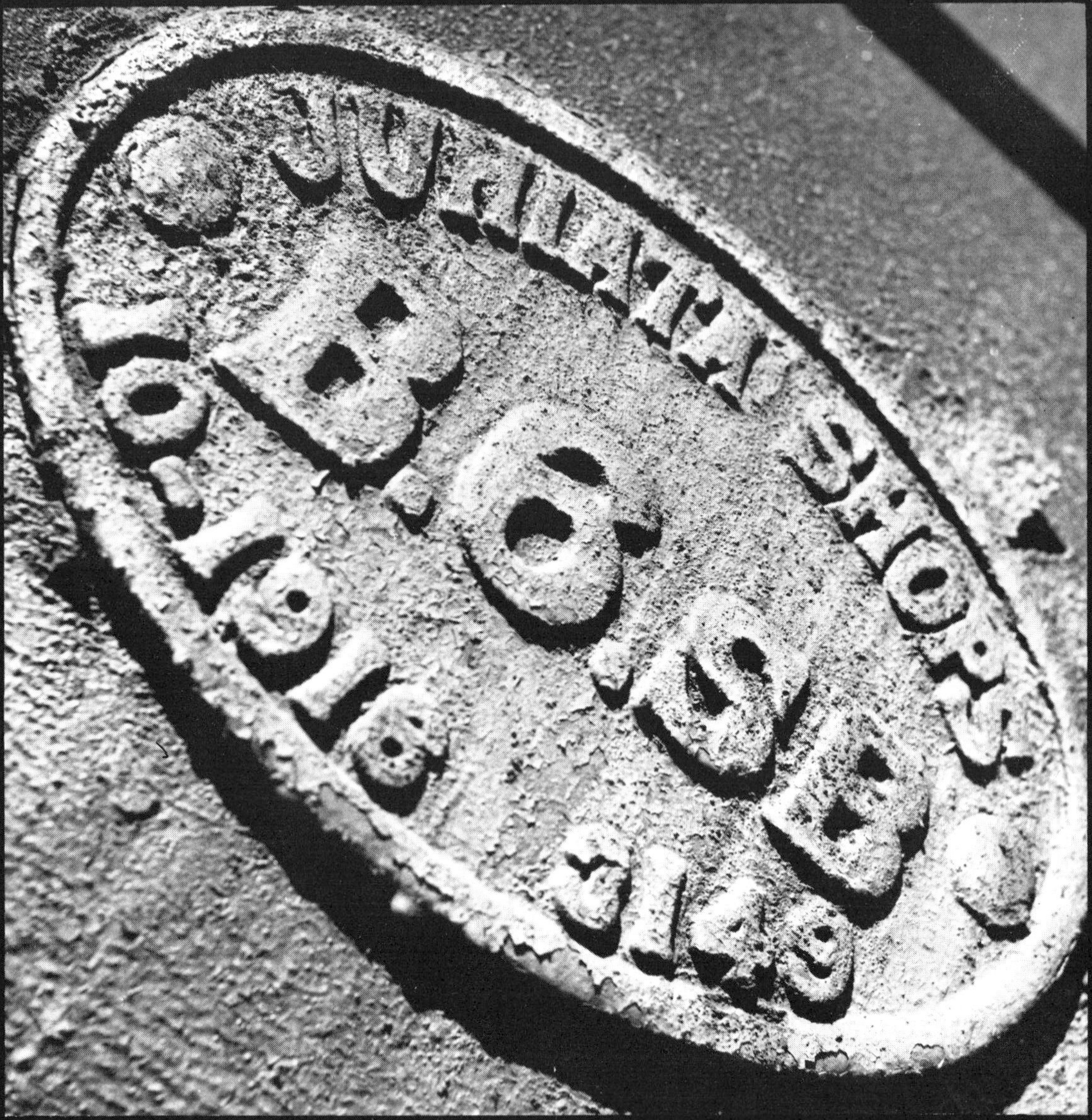

Great steam pictorial

3

Steel flanged wheels on steel ribbons of rails spanning our continent from coast to coast . . . signals, lone sentinels beckoning ever onward the rush of a train . . . relays clicking in CTC sub-stations . . . vast classification yards, with switchers shoving strings of cars . . . rows and rows of crowded tracks . . . massive, hissing steam engines marching from the roundhouse to the ready tracks . . . trains and crews inbound and outbound; and out across the prairie and over the mountains, men and machines working. The local depot . . . the agent and telegraph operator . . . the towerman . . . the pulse-quickening expectancy of an arriving train! Past your backyard . . . down at the end of your street . . . on the outskirts of town . . . and far away on the horizon, the mighty steam locomotives were very much in evidence.

Across the Pacific, and in Europe, the war-making machinery of two powerful nations was in high gear. Newspaper headlines told of our proud Pacific fleet destroyed and our homeland threatened. A black and bleak hour: time to tighten our belts.

Those steel ribbons of rails glinted in the sun; those signals beckoned, and everywhere the pulse-beat of big steam could be felt. In a short time our railroads quadrupled their passenger traffic, hauling more than 97 per cent of all troops; and even more impressive, over 90 per cent of all military hardware. For 45 months our nation's rails worked their finest hour. From farms and factories, mines and refineries, the steel rails carried the burden, keeping the supplies on the move.

The railroads were ready to do whatever Uncle Sam asked of them—and out of Lima, Baldwin, and American Locomotive, and out of some of the railroads' own erecting shops, came incredibly large, high-horsepower steam locomotives, each tailored to tackle the toughest operating conditions with speed in mind. The fireboxes on the modern steamers were so large that supporting four-wheel trailing trucks became commonplace, along with 70-inch and 80-inch drivers. The finest personification of power appeared in the form of giant articulated locomotives, or "two engines in one," having double sets of drivers and cylinders, and utilizing one enormously long boiler. Here was the perfect compromise between a maximum power plant and existing clearance limitations. The art of building steam locomotives had reached its zenith, and for the time being steam would still remain king.

In the years following the war the railroads continued to improve their physical plants, continued to buy and build bigger and faster locomotives, and to increase their tonnage-carrying capacities at higher speeds. The mighty steam locomotives seemed to enjoy an endless youth, even as they welcomed newer and more modern brethren to the rails.

The "great motive-power renaissance" had begun... and for steam, the final curtain was going up on the last big show. In steam's battle for survival, records (and hearts) were broken, and thousands were at trackside to witness "the greatest show on earth." What follows is an across-the-country look at the mightiest of steam locomotives—all working their grandest hours.

623
623

Maine Central's rarely photographed Portland Division afforded some of the most exciting mountain railroading in the east. To get a good-sized train over the White Mountains no fewer than two, and sometimes even three, steam locomotives were assigned. At St. Johnsbury, Vt., Phil Hastings caught 2-8-2s Nos.623 and 616 just after they were cut off their train. St. Johnsbury and Lamoille County's runty 0-6-0 No.22 looks over at the big fellows.

The Central Vermont's lumbering 2-10-4s had the Yankee distinction of being the largest steam locomotives in New England; and to feel one of them passing by certainly hammered home this fact. Here, ponderous T-1b No.703 rolls tonnage through beautiful Vermont back country north of Brattleboro. It's spring, and the geese are winging their way north.

The great north woods of New Hampshire are a rolling wilderness of waterways and forests, accessible in many places only by canoe. Here is where one goes to hunt, hike, boat and, if lucky, reach a clearing to see a hard-working train. In a setting familiar to a few hunters and Maine Central's headend crews, a lone 2-8-2 urges 33 box cars upgrade.

In 1940, Boston & Maine placed three R-1c class 4-8-2s into freight service. They had 73-inch drivers that also enabled them to handle heavy passenger trains. With the exception of almost identical engines ordered in 1935, all heavy freight power were either 61-inch drivered 2-10-2s or 63-inch drivered 2-8-4s. These big Baldwins broke with tradition!

The crack of B & M's Pacific No.3635 cuts through the salty sea air of Manchester, Mass., getting the Boston-bound train underway. The wind is out of the northeast and the lobstermen will not tend their pots this raw day. In the cab, the sashes are drawn tight against the wintry blasts.

Only in traditional New England could the anachronistic Mogul feel at home in the presence of the classic spires of Bulfinch and Wren. The lingering charm of New England and the sturdy little 2-6-0 Moguls unite in Peterboro Village, N.H., at the end of Boston & Maine's 52-mile branch from Worcester.

The Green Mountain Flyer has arrived in Rutland, Vt., from Montreal, and Boston & Maine's Pacific No.3704 backs down to take over on the Boston section. Rutland Railway's green and gold 4-8-2 that came down on the *Flyer* will continue on to Bennington and Troy with the westbound section.

The New Haven, a railroad run on tradition, made it a practice to honor retiring engineers on their last run. Engines were painted, fitted with flags and a sign commemorating the years of service. Engineer George Benard waves farewell as fireman Lou Jerald handles *The Senator* out of Boston's South Station. The locomotive is one of New Haven's standard 1916-built I-4 Pacifics. Across the page, Boston & Albany's Hudson No.611, fresh from a West Albany Shop overhaul, arrives at Boston Terminal with Train No.48 from Springfield. This is the view from the windows of Tower One, just out of the terminal—a favorite spot for photographers.

BOSTON & ALBANY

On this spread are photographic vignettes of the New Haven in steam. High stepping I-4 No.1358 bounds along towards New London with a shoreline local. Engineer Bill Allen keeps the 79-inch drivers in stride ahead of the following *Merchants Limited.*

The Waterbury local rates a big R-3 class 4-8-2 this day and wastes no time laying into a curve along the Naugatuck River. She'll return to Cedar Hill on symbol DN-1 making better use of her 71,000 lbs. tractive effort.

A mighty goliath in the rail yard was New Haven's three-cylindered Y-4 class 0-8-0. These eight-wheel switchers were built in 1924-1927 for hump-yard and transfer service. The 57-inch drivered 3604 simmers at Cedar Hill yard.

Power for the Maybrook line was usually an L-1 class 2-10-2. The original 1918 graduate of a class of fifty Ls, No.3200, clears the Poquag, N.Y. cut with symbol OA-4. The engineer has her hooked-up in the company notch and listens to her stack.

On the following pages, two graceful Delaware & Hudson class J Challengers shrug off a miserable cold rain, laying on the Lanesboro, Pa. wye for helper duty up to Ararat. Don't let their trim lines fool you; these two know how to slug it out on tonnage.

1527

As a photographer, I try to avoid the popular three-quarter "wedge" shot that shows just the engine and train at speed. But who could resist trying it on New York Central's famed 4-track "water level route." By pre-arrangement with the crew at Harmon, wiped-down J-3a Hudson No.5420 provides plenty of smoke north of Oscawanna, N.Y. on her last run out of Harmon. In later years, the J-3s were equipped with giant 14-wheel PT-4 tenders that held forty-six tons of coal and weighed in at a whopping 337,400 lbs. when two-thirds loaded!

After I moved to New York, the New York Central, New Haven and nearby New Jersey roads became my railroad universe. My favorite Central engines by far were the last series L-4b Lima-built Mohawks. In the view above, No.3148 hurries Manhattan-bound perishables through Oscawanna. The "elephant ear" smoke lifters were a Central hallmark. In the lower picture, a sprightly K-3 pacific bounds down the main through Cold Spring, N.Y. with a local from Poughkeepsie.

DUNWOODIE

One of the most picturesque lines in the greater New York area was New York Central's Putnam division from Yorktown Heights into High Bridge, in the Bronx, where commuters had to change trains for mid-town Manhattan. Standard power on the "Put" was the 4-6-0 ten-wheeler, but occasionally a K-class Pacific, or even an ex-B & A Hudson would make the 36-mile run on holiday weekend trains. In an almost rural-like setting, an in-bound mid-morning train slows for Dunwoodie, just eight miles from the Bronx terminus. Today, the "Put" is a weed-covered single track with a once-a-day freight running the 18 miles to Elmsford.

When we had a beautiful day and some free time, a friend and I would go into New York City and take the Liberty Street Ferry over to the Jersey City Terminal where the Jersey Central met the bumper posts. From there, we would ride to Bound Brook and commence hiking to outlying locations to photograph trains. As late as the winter and spring of 1952, the CNJ's rails were loaded with steam. At the upper left, one of a group of the original Pacifics ordered from Baldwin in 1918, P-43 No.822, highballs with a clean stack down the well-ballasted main. Below left, a handsome M-63 class Mikado swings off on to the Philadelphia line with the high cars. Jersey Central's engine-class designations begin with the capital letter of the wheel arrangement, followed by two numbers signifying thousands of pounds of tractive effort. Thus, the M-63 was a Mikado developing 63,000 lbs. tractive effort. The trademark of the CNJ, of course, were the unique center-cabbed camelbacks (or "Mother Hubbards") whose design placed the engineer on the side of the boiler and the fireman aft, shoveling. T-38 class No.772 slams under a Pennsy branch a few minutes off schedule, with some late-morning Gotham-bound patrons at ballast-scorching speed.

772
360

The only area steam represented here that I came to know were Erie's manicured Pacifics, used in suburban service out of Jersey City. Surefooted and trim K-1 No.2559 hustles out-bound commuters across the meadows, near Secaucus, N.J. in 1952. In typical Erie fashion, the 4-6-2's Russian iron boiler jacket is well wiped, and the boards freshly trimmed in white.

What the Erie apparently lacked in appeal, it made up with the devoted allegiance of those who knew her. It was no coincidence that the most dedicated Erie photographers and fans were employees. Tonnage was moved with a vengeance and no bones were made about shippers having priority over passengers. The essence of Erie is frozen in the motion of storming 2-8-4 No.3366 heading hotshot 89 into the reverse curve at Waldwick, N.J.

One of the lesser-known railroads in the area is the New York Susquehanna and Western, whose rails do not venture beyond New Jersey. The road was once Erie property and at that time sixteen low-drivered 2-10-0 Decapods built for Russia in 1918 (but never shipped) were the prime freight haulers. When the "Susie-Q" became independent, only two of the "Deks" were kept. Bob Collins bagged the 2443 at Smiths Mills in January, 1941.

The history of the New York Ontario & Western is a hapless one at best. The locomotives were decrepit and online coal mines unhealthy; passenger business was limited to summer tourism and a proposed Lake Ontario port never materialized. Bridge traffic seemed to be the only route to survival, and some 4-8-2s were ordered. Here, Y-2 No.459 slams through Stony Ford, N.Y. on March 7, 1942 with a war-materiel-laden freight of 95 cars.

Deep in the scenic Warwick Valley, hidden away in the dense woodlands of New Jersey, is the trackage of the 85-mile Lehigh & Hudson River Railway. Tucked in such sylvan surroundings and limited to a short line-distance, this railroad remained relatively obscure to photographers. But what the line lacked in distance, she made up for in size. Witness *(below)* leviathan Consolidation No.90, shaking the heavens, working 101 cars of symbol freight AO-3 into the Warwick, N.Y. yards, the head brakeman up high for rear end signals. At right, heading out of Warwick, the big handsome 4-8-2 No.10 booms throaty exhausts as the hogger carefully widens on her, with well over 100 empty hoppers bound for Phillipsburg and the nearby bituminous coal fields. If we could shoot it in steam all over again, I'm sure I would find plenty of company along the L&H!

The Lackawanna depended on big 4-8-4s for freight and was one of the first roads to employ this great wheel arrangement, ordering twenty of them in 1929. The 4-8-4, generally called the Northern type, was known as a Pocono on the Lackawanna. One is shown getting underway out of Point Morris, N.J., with empties west, back to the mines.

In mid-January, 1948, Lackawanna's Pacific (whose number could not be identified by nearly-frozen photographer John Pickett) heads passenger train No.1903 from Binghamton on the Syracuse division, a few miles away from the division's namesake city. Obviously, the 4-6-2 had recently raised hell with a snow bank.

Reading's fat-boilered 2-10-2 No.3004 pours forth 92,500 lbs. tractive effort in moving a train up through Locust Gap, Pa., in July, 1953. This engine, along with nine others, was rebuilt by Reading from a compound Mallet 2-8-8-2. The proverbially frugal Pennsylvania Dutch saved money on this home-built! At the right is Starrucca Viaduct, called by many "the eighth wonder of the world." Built in 1848 by a Scotch Civil Engineer, James Kirkwood, the Roman-styled structure is 1,200 feet long and 110 feet high. It still stands and can support the millions of pounds of two passing trains. Bob Collins was lucky enough to be there in the days of steam. Below right, Lehigh Valley's big T-1 class 4-8-4 No.5100 works eastward through Mountain Top, Pa., with a clear board, clean fire, and a good head of steam. This Elesco feedwater-equipped brute was built by Baldwin in 1938 and started a 4-8-4 bandwagon for many a railroad as World War Two broke out.

W
W

IAN'S
SH
ED
RES

Western Maryland was a must for steam photographers. Apart from running through some of the most beautiful country in the east, the road possessed distinctly individualistic power, well-maintained and beautifully painted. On the left page, seen toward the end of a career, WM's husky 2-8-0 No.762 darkens the sunny skies with a drumstick plume, making an entrance into Elkins, W. Va. on an otherwise quiet Sabbath. At right, the hills come alive with the thunderous movement of Western Maryland's WM-1 over the Alleghenies. It took no less than two big Baldwin M-2 Challengers and an equally ponderous Decapod on the rear to move the 78 heavily loaded cars. Twin stacked No.1204 leads the early morning parade up through Corriganville, Md. on August 24, 1952.

JACKSON BEAUTY SUPPLY CO.

At left, Southern's apple green ("Virginia green") and gold pin-striped PS-4 No.1398 barks out of Greensboro, N.C. with the Atlanta-bound *Piedmont Limited* in 1946. All Southern's premium trains rated these elegant engines. Eastern neighbor Atlantic Coast Line was one of the few railroads to use the 4-6-2 Pacific in freight service; usually it hauled passengers. Also deviating from standard practice, the road usually specified smaller drivers on its Pacifics. Two exceptions were both of the AJ-2 class 73-inch drivered heavy Pacifics that came from the Great Northern. Above right, Belpaire-boilered No.7153 is on the lead with P-5a Pacific 1528, charging into Stratford, Ga., with the extra heavy consist of the *Dixie Flagler* in 1949.

An engine I regret never having seen was the Atlantic Coast Line R-1 class 4-8-4. This Baldwin, judging from photos, had to be about the most handsome steam power in the south. Below right, 80-inch drivered No.1810 lays over in Richmond, Va. on call for the *Florida Special* in 1940.

5043

Baltimore & Ohio's power was classically elegant, whatever the wheel arrangement. The road was always a "second-class rival" as far as giants Pennsy and New York Central were concerned, but in my view, the B & O had a charismatic appeal that no other railroad possessed. At the left, train No.21, the *Washingtonian* hammers up past Manila tower and in a second will blast into Manila tunnel. She's assaulting Cranberry Grade and P-1d No.5043 is making no bones about it. The large capacity sand dome attests to her mountain domain. Above, a long-barreled "Big Six" talks it up through the interlocking at Hancock, Md. with a mile of train stretched out behind her drawbar.

To the visitor, the Alleghenies are pure scenic grandeur; to the native, they are respected for the rich black seams of bituminous coal that abound below the surface; to the B & O's operating department in the early 1940s, with a railroad strained with war tonnage, they were a headache of major proportions.

On these pages, two oil trains make their slow, thunderous passage over the Alleghenies behind toiling, tireless 2-8-8-0s. On the rear, as was the usual practice, two more plodding 2-8-8-0s shoulder against the steel caboose, sanding, steaming, sweating.

One of the most massive, most powerful and heaviest steam locomotives ever built was Lima's super-power 2-6-6-6 Allegheny, constructed for the Chesapeake & Ohio and neighboring Virginian after the war. This fine locomotive was the pinnacle of the builder's art and the embodiment of brute strength.

My first acquaintance with the Allegheny was in 1951 on a rainy afternoon in Fostoria, Ohio; the awesome impression they made on me is still very vivid. In May of 1947, Tom Donahue was witness to two of these 1,152,000 pound brutes, fore and aft, on a coal train eastbound through Ronceverte, W. Va.

Pennsy came to town with just about everything they had to offer—certainly the biggest variety of steam locomotives in the Windy City. Across the page and above, double-slotted K-4s Nos.2032 and 5496 arrive with the in-bound *Broadway Limited* in October 1943; at near right, Pennsy's unique direct-drive steam turbine No.6200 arrives in Chicago with the heavy *Gotham Limited* in 1946. This revolutionary "dream turbine" was constructed out of a strong faith in steam and an allegiance to on-line coal operators. Pennsy's ultimate chapter in steam was written by 26 fabulous Q-2 class 4-4-6-4s. They developed 8,000 horsepower, steamed easily, and were as easy to fire as a stoker-equipped 2-8-2. At far right No.6190 steams quietly on the ready track next to K-4 No.5432. Even at rest, the big duplex-drive locomotive carried its one million pounds exceptionally well.

PENNSYLVANIA
2032
BANGOR & AROOSTOOK

The Gary, Hammond, Calumet City industrial complex is probably the most powerful concentration of industry in America. Steel mills, coke ovens, railroad tracks, tin plate works, bulk oil fields, power lines, sludge piles and trucks are everywhere. Yet this ugly maze is a fascinating backdrop—and also a challenge for the rail photographer. Here, a New York Central K-3n Pacific accelerates away from a board in East Chicago. Below, seen in 1947, one of Chicago and North Western's 250 daily trains rattles and bangs through and over the interlocking into North Western Station with morning commuters in tow. The view of Pacific No.547 is out the window of the Lake Street Tower where, during the morning and evening rush hours, it was common practice to control the consecutive moves of a half dozen moving trains. The class E Pacific was the standard suburban engine on the C&NW.

A provocative pastime of railroaders, buffs and modelers is debating who built the best, the most handsome, the most powerful locomotives for their size—and which ones were utilized most efficiently. In my judgment, top honors go to New York Central's magnificent Niagaras. Something to ponder—No.6000, the original of its class, totaled 52,525 miles in two months on the 15-car heavyweight *Commodore Vanderbilt* between Harmon, N.Y. and Chicago, averaging 56.2 m.p.h. over the 925 mile run.

This shot of 6012 arriving in Chicago with the twenty-two car *Pacemaker* shows off the Niagara's straight, functional lines. The "elephant ears" are for lifting smoke and the huge 14-wheel tender is almost dwarfed! Pictured below is a Chicagoland favorite, one of Burlington's home-built 0-5a Northerns. Ray Buhrmaster caught No.5635 roaring west through Belmont Station, Ill., on April 26, 1951.

Of all the railroads, Missouri Pacific stayed with the most puritanical approach to steam locomotive design. No shrouds nor painted stripes nor fireballs, just classically-proportioned power. Above, outside Sedalia, Mo., in March, 1948, No.1310 pulls into the hole for the *Eagle*. Nature's cloud spread casts its spell over the pastoral Missouri countryside. At the upper right, the crew in sister No.1316 hastens their freight on a "skin run" ahead of the *Eagle,* picking up "19s" on the fly at Sandy Hook, Mo., in June, 1948. This way freight originally had orders to run ahead of the *Eagle* as far as Sedalia, but lost time in switching. Now he has to get into the clear in a hurry! At the lower right, pictured in the following March, the un-thawed fields await the arrival of Spring; the harrow and the plow. It's business as usual for the Mop, and the heavy 4-8-2 No.5336 heading a red ball through Otterville, Mo., was surely heard—and hopefully seen.

1316

5336

Big fellow. In the Thirties, the management of the Kansas City Southern was sensitive to the increasing demands of on-line shippers for higher speed freight service and several of the 2-8-8-0 mallets were converted from compound to simple locomotives. The re-built mallets began to move tonnage with a vengeance and in many cases attained a 50% increase in speed. The expensive conversions temporarily answered the need, but longer freights were desired and management turned to Lima and the drawing boards for an engine that could roll plenty of tonnage at high speed. The zenith of steam power on the KCS was epitomized in ten clean and handsome Texas types built in 1937 by the Lima Locomotive Works. Fresh from the back shop, the original class J, No.900, pumps air into her train at Kansas City, prior to heading down the main to De Queen, Arkansas, in March, 1951.

With "Frisco Faster Freight" emblazoned on her tank, Frisco's 4-8-4 No.4504 races war tonnage through the early Missouri dawn, more than living up to her proud slogan. These war-built 4-8-4s were built for an obvious job, and also relieved many tired ranks of older Mikados and 4-8-2s for less exacting duty.

928

At 12:45 p.m., the *Mills City Limited* threads its way out of Kansas City Union Station during a mid-day lull. The leisurely schedule calls for a mid-morning arrival at Minneapolis-St. Paul. The magnificent Union Station was opened on October 30, 1914; today, daily public tours are conducted through the all but deserted massive structure by the Kansas City chapter of the American Institute of Architects. We can thank Don Smith for returning us to happier days.

9079

40
5109

My early trackside travels were strictly limited by leg endurance and foot callouses! With a bicycle, my railroad explorations expanded considerably. After a stop at the depot for the "line-up" I would pick a destination on the joint trackage of the U.P. and Rock Island for a day of trains. At the below left, *The Kansan* blasts eastward out of Lawrence behind a loud Sweeney-stacked Harriman Pacific and meets a whistle-saluting Rock Island R-1 Northern slowing her freight for a water stop. Upper left, on January 21, 1951, this job picked up orders, but didn't stop for water. She's heading west in the early morning light and will run on into Topeka for water. In a moment, the agent back at the depot will be hooping up "19's" to the rear end and the "nine" will "widen on her" down the flat tangent track. Toward evening, and a mile west of Lawrence *(above)*, the hog-head on this eastbound has the 9043 hooked-up under a glorious plume of smoke. For me, a favorite locomotive was a fitting end to a perfect day.

Lawrence is surrounded by rolling, rich farmlands whose crops have withstood the blistering suns of August and the driven snow of winter for decades. In the summer of 1951, the heavens opened up, the Kaw River rose and the area was hit by the worst floods in its history. The crops did not survive, nor did the Santa Fe trackage where Bob Olmsted made this dramatic picture of Santa Fe's huge No.3780 waiting in the drenching rain for a highball out of Lawrence. In another week, the Santa Fe would be across the river on the higher U.P. tracks. The previous February, and in better days, Santa Fe's towering 4-8-4 No.2908 *(shown opposite)*, approaches Olathe, Kansas, with westbound tonnage—its smoke-lifting stack extension a hallmark of the road's operating department.

2908

With no fewer than ten major railroads, Omaha was a paradise for train lovers. Rails radiated into and out of Omaha, crossing hill-and-dale terrain quite unique for a Plains state. Native Bill Kratville, railroader and photographer, concentrated his genius in and around Omaha. In these vignettes *(below left)*, Bill caught Missouri Pacific's handsome MK-63 Mike No.1524 working freight north into Omaha—her reverse yoke shoved forward and her clean, sharp exhaust lifting high. At right, Union Pacific's X9028 west bangs under the Dahlman Avenue overpass with an awesome report after cresting the grade out of town. Ten miles west of Omaha in the little town of Elkhorn, *(above left)*, the icy morning stillness is shattered by a husky pair of U.P. regulars charging west under a mantle of frosty steam. This Christmas card photo was taken on December 25, 1951.

N.R.C.
19331

TEXAS & PACIFIC
908

Texas and Pacific's management stuck to a "no-nonsense" policy as far as locomotive appearance was concerned. All T & P locomotives remained conspicuously groomed with burnished rods, nickel-steel cylinder heads and brass-capped stacks. At left above, the morning light glints softly off the contours of M-2 No.908, assigned to the westbound *Texan,* as she backs into the Dallas station. A real celebrity on the Rio Grande was the Baldwin L-105 dual-service 4-6-6-4. One of these long-boilered greyhounds romps along through the upper Utah desert, near Thompson, with a mere 57 cars on June 30, 1941 *(below).*

Many times you notch the throttle—listen and feel—yank it another notch—lean out and feel—make sure you don't slip and lose your momentum. Above right, the hogger on this great Rio Grande 2-8-8-2 is doing just that, skillfully getting his heavy train up out of Minturn, Colo. The fireboy is contributing by keeping a good head of steam and a clean fire. Below, the fireman calls signals on the pots as the engineer walks big 4-8-2 No.901 through the leads and back towards the waiting *Southerner* for El Paso.

9005

Out on the upper plains of Nebraska and Wyoming, the towns are widely spaced, the land is flat, and homesteaders and ranchers are few and far between. There's usually a wind and always a good chance for the weather to take a quick, violent turn for the worse. There is nothing to delay or tempt the traveler—that is, unless it's a distant train such as Union Pacific's X9005 west. The smoke can be seen for miles, the shrill whistle heard occasionally when the wind dies down, and then the wagontop boilered 4-12-2 approaches on another train's markers, making a service (brake) application, then running with a drifting throttle, waiting for the red eyes on the boards to go yellow. Fifty to a hundred miles or more back, a chain of fast-moving thunderstorms looms on the horizon. At the right, Union Pacific's 4-8-4 No.832 majestically blasts out of Denver with the daily *San Francisco Overland.* On this March, 1942, departure, the train has an extra heavy consist of headend revenue and cars of troops bound for the coast. Below, Dick Kindig documented two of Santa Fe's great 74-inch drivered 2-10-4s booming forth in splendor on the climb near Abo, N.M., with an eastbound green fruit block in October, 1947. This great railroad, with these great engines, never needed articulated power to conquer the west.

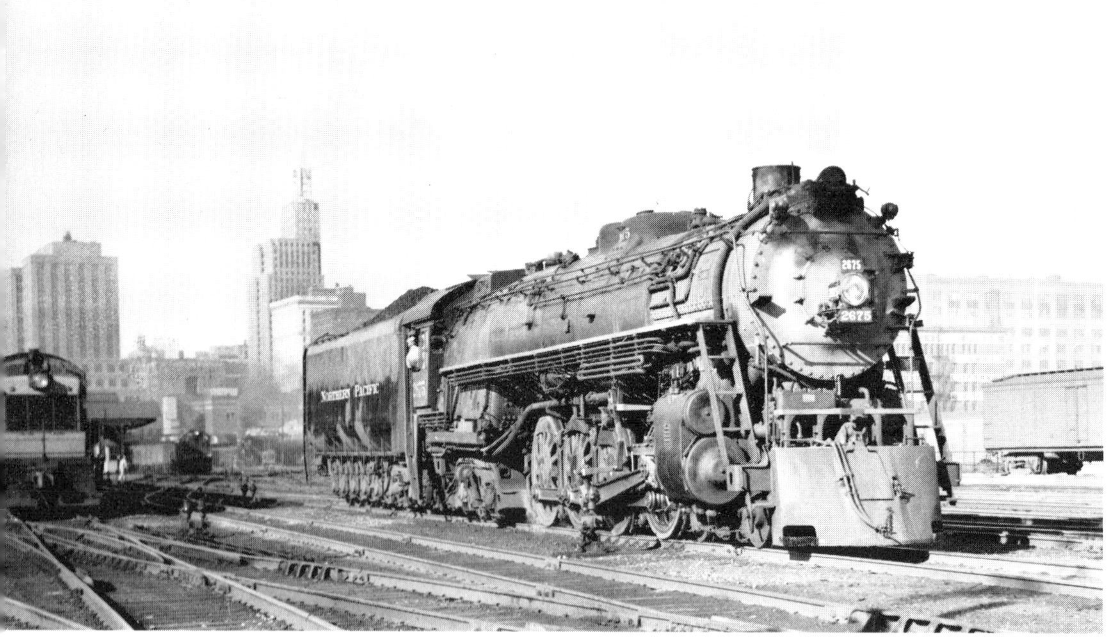

Northern Pacific was the line that bought the famous roller bearing Timken No.1111 "Four Aces" 4-8-4 back in 1926 and thus pioneered the modern wheel arrangement called "Northern." Over the years, the N.P. kept ordering, improving and re-ordering Northern types, with the last two orders going to Baldwin in 1941 and 1943 for eighteen identical A-4 and A-5 class 4-8-4s. These pictures are a salute to a beautiful Northern—one that normally ran from St. Paul, Minnesota to Livingston, Montana, a record-breaking 1800 mile run for a coal-burning locomotive. Above, No.2670 leaves St. Paul Terminal with a troop extra carrying white. The Johnson bar is in the corner and her cylinder cocks wide open in a rapid departure. At the left, the magnificent lines of this locomotive are revealed as she backs her fourteen-wheeled tender down to the waiting *North Coast Limited.* At the right, a boiler-top view from St. Paul's 4th Street bridge.

2677

4020

To most people, Idaho is noted for its potatoes and broad rolling sheep pastures, just as the Northern Pacific is known by most railroaders as "The Main Street of the Northwest." One little-known branch of the N.P., however, offered a profile that forced ponderous 2-8-8-2s down on their hands and knees with a lean 600 ton train! From Wallace to Lookout, the single iron twisted and turned and tangled with the worst conditions the Bitterroots had to offer. As evidenced in Hank Griffith's beautiful portrait of N.P.'s eastbound thirteen-car train through the Coeur d'Alene Mountains, the tangent offered a running start for the tortuous climb ahead. At the upper right is a locomotive little known to most railfans—Great Northern's M-2 class Belpaire boilered 2-6-8-0. No.1973 whips along on the point of an oil train, leaving her white calling card of condensed steam behind. The photograph at lower right was also made in the beautiful Big Sky country of Montana. It's a cool, crisp, sunny day in Glacier National Park and Great Northern's N-3 class 2-8-8-0 No.2005 makes a lovely scene departing Whitefish, Mont., on the way west to pick up a troop train. Her round Vanderbilt tank was designed to prevent water "slosh" on starts, stops and curves.

2553
GREAT NORTHERN

A railroad photographer's dream come true: Great Northern's green-jacketed S-1 class 4-8-4 No.2553 rolls splendidly west under a billowing canopy of soot, looking for all the world like a table-top model. No phone poles to cope with, no trees in the way—just a clear Montana sky on a perfect day. All the ingredients are here; the weathered old hack, the generator plume, the rods at full stroke and the ashcat leaning way out. For this caboose hop, it's a green board west of Minot! Below, in a similar setting, a Great Northern 2-8-8-2 drums across the huge Gassman Coulee Bridge three miles west of Minot, N.D. Not many railroads courted photographers during the war, but by pre-arrangement, this accommodating crew furnished plenty of smoke for photographer Jack Pontin. Upper right, and in another model perspective, Oregon & Northwestern's 2-8-2 No.1400 comes out of the woods with a bulbous load of logs south of Trout Creek, Oregon. Lower right, Northern Pacific's mountain climbing Challenger No.5136 urges a mile of tonnage up Bozeman Pass in Montana. On the rear is 2-8-8-4 No.5003. These high-stepping, barnstorming Challengers commanded much respect—and higher crew pay from management. This rugged breed roamed across the Missouri Valley, Yellowstone, and the Continental Divide.

900
900 900

It was a lucky photographer who came face to face with an articulating boiler—in perfect sunlight—while the locomotive was at rest! Phil Hastings caught Spokane, Portland & Seattle's awesome Z class 4-6-6-4 Challenger laying over on a slight curving track of the Hillyard engine terminal at Spokane in 1950.

One usually associates the majestic High Sierras and winding Feather River with the Western Pacific Railroad. To no lesser extent, one conjures up the sight of giant articulateds snaking along countless canyons overlooking the turbulent Feather River. A seldom photographed segment of the W.P. is the back country Niles Canyon area of California. Above right, a big camera shy MK-60 Mikado No.308 makes up for any disappointment in the scenery as she works time freight No.62 eastbound near Sunol in Spring 1948. This 2-8-2 was equally at home utilizing her 71,300 lbs. tractive effort in pusher service. Over in Idaho, in the northern part of the state, is the Camas Prairie Railroad. The total mainline trackage is 149 miles and the line is jointly operated by both Northern Pacific and Union Pacific. On any given day, power from either or both roads can be operated. On this June 11th, 1954 day, the train to Headquarters *(below right)* is in the knuckled-grip of smoke belching Union Pacific 2-8-2 No.2703 departing Orfino, Idaho.

Far removed from Southern Pacific's vast California service, a ponderous AC-12 cab-forward mallet clomps up grade through the Nevada desert out of Fernley with the *Northwest Special.* This line, called the Modoc line, provides a "back door" gateway into the Northwest through Alturas to Klamath Falls. The mallet's unique design afforded excellent vision for head end crews and eliminated the danger of smoke asphyxiation in the snowsheds and tunnels that thread the High Sierras. At right, a trip worthy of a vista dome is Camas Prairie's line along the roaring, trout-filled Orofino Creek towards Headquarters, Idaho. We're riding on a flat and the galloping low-drivered 2-8-2 is trailing a white feathery plume, in stark contrast to the backdrop of the towering firs. The lettering on the tank identifies this U.P. engine as coming from subsidiary Los Angeles & Salt Lake.

L.A.&S.L.
2703

5093
5093

California! For those of us east of the Rockies, the thought of going west to see what was considered to be the most spectacular railroading in America held the same attraction as the lure of gold to the early 49ers. On these pages, I have staked my claims to four different phases of rugged, California mainline railroading. At far left above, Santa Fe's enormous 4-8-4 No.3777 comes in off the desert near Hesperia amidst Joshua trees and manzanita and starts the westward attack on the San Bernardino and San Gabriel mountains towards Los Angeles. These great engines thought nothing of running the 1765 miles between Kansas City, and L.A. and sometimes the 2227 miles from Chicago without change. These outstanding record-breaking runs earned them the reputation of long-distance champions —and perhaps the finest locomotives ever built. At far left below, Bill Barham caught the eastward assault of U.P.'s 2-10-2 No.5093 and 4-8-4 No.829 double-heading the *Los Angeles Limited* up the long Cajon climb toward Summit and Victorville. On this page, two scenes typical of Southern Pacific's empire; *(above left)* an AC cab forward 4-8-8-2 pulls out onto the main with a Coast Line manifest under a volcanic outburst of boiling oily exhaust. The fireman has evidently "dusted her flues out" with sand. At lower left, *The San Joaquin Daylight* drifts down off the Tehachapis, northbound, in a cloud of hot brakeshoe smoke.

They also serve who only stand and wait...

4

For me, there was always a special kind of magic about the roundhouse, and any opportunity to visit one was certainly more than welcomed. It was a chance to get to know intimately the great locomotives which we were accustomed to seeing out on the railroad. The roundhouse was almost always tucked away in some far corner of town, but was revealed by the haze of smoke overhead. As you approached, the huge coaling dock stood above the smoking engines—dominating everything else in the yard. The supporting servicing structures for steam were just about as fascinating as the locomotives themselves.

As you approached the cindery grounds near the roundhouse, the air had a pungent smell that no dyed-in-the-wool railroader could ever forget. Before you stood the great curving walls of the roundhouse, with huge window panes and head lighted boiler fronts looking out, and incredible noises from within. The eagerness to find a back door, slide it open and go inside this great and wonderful place was overwhelming.

If you were ever inside a roundhouse, it was an experience you'll never forget. Inside this cavernous home, the first thing that struck you was the size of the locomotives! Close up...right next to you! And the noise! Everywhere you could hear the banging and pounding of hammers, the *chit-chat, chit-chat* of alemite guns, and the ear-splitting hiss of steam. A whistle from a far stall echoed through the murky air, and the roar from open cylinder cocks could be heard as an engine backed out onto the turntable. Most of the engines remained in their stalls for routine inspections, some for boiler washouts and repairs, others simply awaiting their assignments.

The men moving about knew their work; it was their life! Each knew the innermost personality of these great engines, and repairs were made without the help of textbooks or intricate machines. A good machinist could make or rebuild a necessary part with the tools readily available in the roundhouse. In some cases an "ailment" could be remedied merely by a few strategic taps with a hammer!

Outside the roundhouse, and across the turntable, locomotives had their fires dumped and cleaned, took on water, coal and sand. Ultimately I would complete my visit by going to the ready track, to photograph the great steamers which were awaiting their call to duty.

Out on the line, and far from the roundhouse, the silent water plugs, tanks and coaling docks stood ready and waiting for their call—grimy guardians that constantly reminded us of the great age of steam.

104
104

Even a distant view of locomotives set my pulse beating a little faster—there they were, just waiting for me. It was hard to hold myself to a walk: it's a cardinal sin you know, to *be seen* running in a railroad yard. The distance does lend enchantment and the shots of all the engines should look great. The yard hostler is building up a head on that Pennsy . . . the fires look clean.

The yard tracks are wet from leaky injectors and fittings; the ties are greasy where exposed above clinkers, ash and cinders; there are many places to step in, or even fall into—always look, and remember to step *over* the rail. Below the towering coaling dock, chains rattle and chutes bang down with the tremendous clatter of coal tumbling into the tender. A bell, cylinder cocks, and another engine moves into line.

5308
B&O

Best time to shoot an engine, when the fire is dirty and the hostler shovels more on to build up steam. The blower is cracked a little, to keep smoke out of the cab while shoveling and to increase draft on the fire. This helps raise the steam pressure. With a signed release in your pocket, the guys usually didn't give a damn as long as you were careful. The urge to get up on the tender and shoot into the gangway was always a great one—and at times brought out the foreman! Best to have a release. I always felt at home in the cab. I loved it! Even sitting on the left hand cushions and looking back at the tender bunker and waiting scoop fascinated me. The absence of coal indicated that someone must have been working on the stoker screw, accessible only through a hatchplate on the floor. The glass indicated 180 lbs., not much of a fire. Here comes the hostler...

Sitting in a cab and reminiscing with the trainmen always created in me a feeling of envy and the sorrowful conviction that I had been born too late, that I had missed out on an era when men and machine depended on each other. Being in *any* cab was great—even at rest. The smell, the inner-life of the machine felt through the soft panting, cab-throbbing air pumps, and the constant sizzling of water dripping on the backhead. Seems like I always watch that steam gauge... sputterings came from a leak somewhere.

"Can you stand back over here? I've gotta throw a few diamonds on the fire... man, it's a helluva lot easier with a stoker... I remember the 5300's before they put 'em in... used to bust our backs out on the road ... there, a nice even bed oughta do it."

"Do you want me to check the water level?"

"Yeah, go ahead, it should be OK."

This kind of conversation went on for hours, and that's what I came for. On the left-hand side, the stoker feed, manifold and blower; on the floor, the fire door activator. On this side, the throttle lever, engine brake, train brake—and the roar of the fire through the open fire doors.

People speak of the steam locomotive as the Iron Horse, but unless they have experienced the unforgettable thrill of opening the throttle and pounding over the rails at 80 miles an hour (feeling the gait and drive of this great machine), they will never know just how meaningful the description is. You've just got to get up on them. You can't see anything through the camera view finder out on the line. Sometimes that last step before getting off is a little tricky—usually it's in a little—always hold tightly to the grab irons. Man! You know the power she has when you look at her wheels ...and how does the rail hold her? What keeps her from flying off the track? Best to get that picture of her running gear before the sun goes in. Sometimes she looks like she's moving when she's not. I guess that's normal with functional machinery. Rods and valve gear exemplified the power.

Cylinder cocks and a bell from a moving engine is nearby. Time really flies and it's getting dark. A cleaner grabs a high pressure steam line to clean an engine's running gear; the hostler climbs aboard another engine to run her onto the table and into the house. There's something almost mystical as the lights go on in the yard and up on the high coaling dock. The murk seems to settle and coal smoke is everywhere—my favorite smell! The sounds of turbo-generators fill the air, an occasional blow down of a water glass, opening of pet cocks and crunching stoker screws. The lights begin to dance on the engines, highlighting the contours and casting eerie light-and-shadow patterns on these great machines. Many are lined up to go into the house. The night crew is on duty now. Sounds of work are clearly heard inside the roundhouse. The first order of business is to introduce myself to the foreman and then stay back, out of his way.

3008

5219
5219

BORE

6012
NEW YORK
CENTRAL
SYSTEM

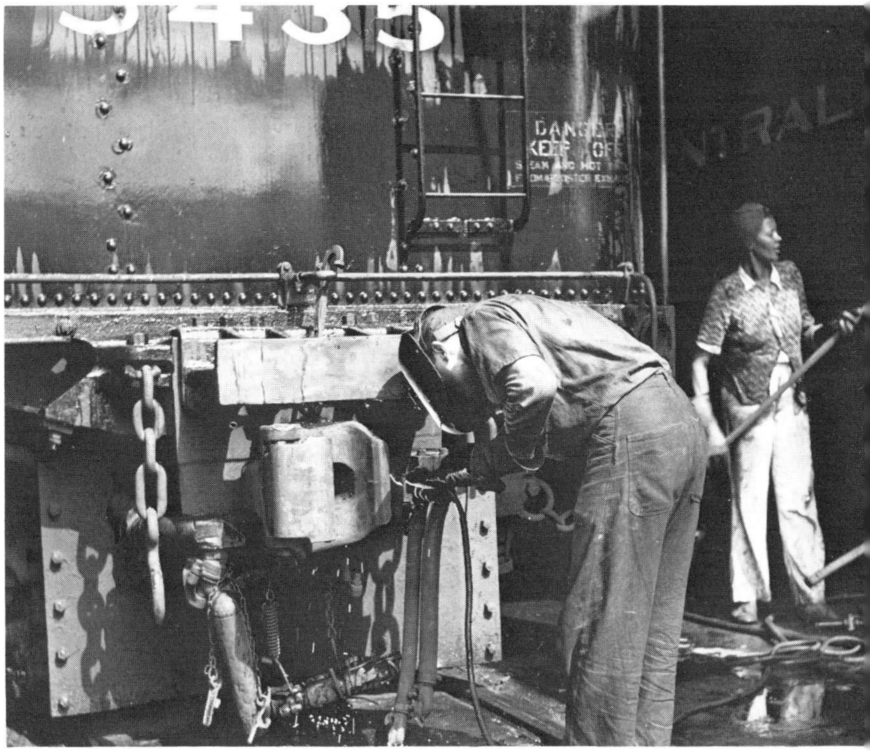

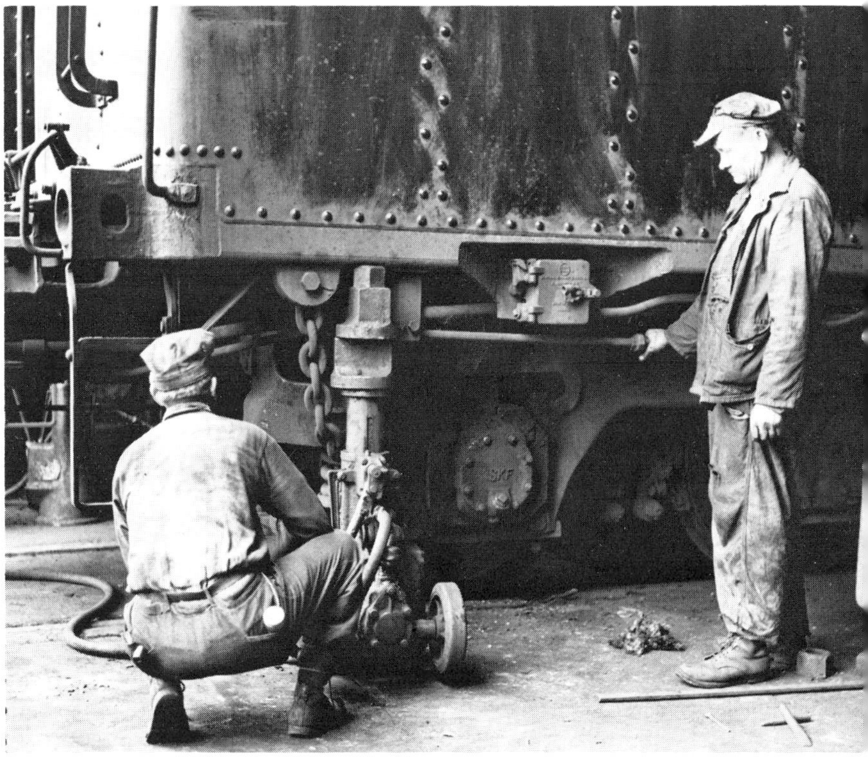

The night shift has begun and several engines are being worked on. Most of them are dead and major repairs are being performed by an army of machinists, pipe fitters, oilers and two blacksmiths. The boiler sheathing and lagging is being removed from that one; a main rod is being taken off on the next track. It would be easy to spend the night, just watching; the Coke machine would keep me going. In the morning more men seemed to be on the job —giving a piston the magna flux test, replacing wedges and shimming couplers. Work on that L-4 has been completed according to the engine report on her pilot. A long whistle just blew and the first trick is coming on—time to squeeze out between that tender and the doorjamb and watch where I step. Lack of sleep doesn't help.

4825
NEW YORK CENTRAL
5249
NEW YORK CENTRAL

I guess the fresh air smells pretty good. The morning light is beautiful, and there isn't a cloud in the sky. The warm sun and cool air feel great! So much to photograph—but three Cokes for supper are hardly enough. Time to get a big breakfast at the diner. Maybe first, up the ladder, very carefully—"damn it!"—very carefully, up to that obscure corner on the lower roof. A whistle sounds and a bell starts clanging—cylinder cocks open, and the rail creaks as a great Hudson backs out onto the table. *Ka-clink, ka-clank, ka-clank.* Back down on the ground again, I feel even more weary. Another Hudson is over there and that warm coffee looks mighty good. Breakfast sounds even better! More engines are coming in off the road, others are being readied, more are spotted on the ready track. An ashpit cleaner is the last guy I'll see for now. At some point, I've got to put temptation behind me. I'll be back—but how to explain my blackface makeup and shiny cameras at the diner?

Certainly no front runners in anyone's popularity poll, but two of my own favorites were the Rock Island and Soo Line 4-8-4s. The "Rock" sired the largest stable of 4-8-4s, while the Soo only had four. The managements of both railroads were happy with these Northerns and clearly attributed their recaptured business to these high-wheeling locomotives. Ray Buhrmaster made these two table studies: Soo's 0-20 at Schiller Park, Ill. and Rock Island's R-67 at Blue Island, Ill.

At Santa Fe's San Bernardino roundhouse, the big 2-10-2 No.3892 rides the turntable to be spotted on the servicing track lead to follow 2-8-0 No.1976. The 3892 has just returned from helper duty on the hill and camera-carrying Santa Fe employee Fletcher Swan immortalized this behind-the-scenes vignette of the Los Angeles Division.

Burlington
Route
6313
C B & Q

Two men have swung open the high wooden doors at the end stall of Burlington's picturesque old roundhouse at Centralia, Ill. and the sounds of steam and a bell come from within. The long tender—and the most handsome of Burlington's locomotives, a 1927 Texas type M-4a, backs onto the table. The men, who have spent their lives with steam, look on admiringly. She'll head a long swaying string of empty hoppers back to Beardstown and the southern Illinois coal mines. On the right, a bell ringer is oiled.

READING

The time-honored stance. Whether in the coal fields of Pennsylvania, farmlands of Illinois, or bayous of Mississippi, the picture was the same. The Iron Horse needed its water. How many of us remember the water plugs ("columns" to some) in our hometown, and waited next to them for a train to arrive. We always enjoyed watching the fireman climb up on the tender, throw open the hatch and grab the long hook to swing the big spout over and down into the tender. The hogger, after oiling around, would get back up on his right hand cushion and watch the glasses.

Up on the tender, it was always exciting and entertaining to oversee a 20,000 gallon drink of water cascading into the hatch. On the right, the morning parade of mine-run assignments congregate on the ready track for their drinks at Peach Creek, W. Va., on the Chesapeake & Ohio in March 1956. No.1331 is a small H-4 class compound mallet 2-6-6-2.

The big old wooden water tank was a familiar symbol of steam railroading and almost always stood out in the middle of nowhere—usually leaking! At the upper right, two of Rio Grande's narrow gauge giants struggle up to the old tank near Cresco, N.M. with an eastbound Chama-Antonito stock extra. Below, Canadian Pacific's 2-8-2 No.5400 works steam and engine brake, easing up to spot for a drink at Harvey, New Brunswick on a St. John-McAdam freight in August, 1959. On the right, Nickel Plate Hudson No.173—head on—pinchhits for a Mike on a Chicago division local to Fort Wayne and takes a drink at Tippecanoe, Ind., in March 1957.

173
173
173

A familiar sight on the North American landscape was the coaling dock out on the line —"rural skyscrapers" as I used to call them. With a car, it was fairly easy to spot one looming on the horizon—first, of course, having inquired about its general location from the local station agent. Above, in an unusual view, Burlington's 01-a No.4967 has just been coaled and topped-off at the Henin Jct. Ill. engine terminal in November, 1957. To the right, train-watching *Trains* Editor David Morgan talks to the head brakeman on the Markham Local as the northbound *Panama Limited* whips past on the Illinois Central main at Gilman, Ill.

Towards the very end of steam, my buddy Karl and I would spread the maps, consult the Official Guide of Railways and draw lines converging on roads that paralled the tracks. We'd pack food in one large box and cameras and film in another—hopefully enough for two weeks! Our first cherished objective was to get to a coaling dock during daylight hours, since they always afforded a good show of working steam. Featured are *(top left)* B&O's beautifully proportioned T-4 No.755 easing 6,291 tons away from the Warwick, Ohio dock behind a skillful hogger who doesn't use sand; *(above)* one of Union Pacific's fat-boilered 2-8-2s chuffing away from the La Salle, Colo., coaling stage, and *(right)* Howard Fogg's backlit view of Union Pacific's mightiest-in-the-land Big Boy No.4016 getting underway eastbound from the Rock River, Wyo. chute with F.E. "Brigham" Young at the throttle. They let this train out ahead of the streamliner fleet and some 65 m.p.h. running was in order! To the left, Canadian National's green trimmed U-1f 4-8-2 starts eighty-nine MTY's out of Portage La Prairie, Manitoba. The octagonal wooden water tank is typical of Canadian National's early railroad architecture.

UNION
PACIFIC
4016

4165

I cannot think of a better, or more fitting, finale to this personal chapter than to conclude it with the brilliant work of two incomparable nighttime railroad photographers, Dick Steinheimer and Jim Shaughnessy. At the left, Dick's look at one of Southern Pacific's cyclopean cab-forwards in the hot darkness of a Colton, Cal. night and above, Jim's yard portrait of Sydney and Louisburg's No.85 trundling past two towering hallmarks of steam in Glace Bay, Nova Scotia.

Diesels– colorful couriers of change

5

By mid-1939, some railroads were acknowledging the colorful diesel's role in passenger service, and to some it was beginning to look as though the diesel had finally established itself in this area of railroading. Over seventy diesel passenger units were in mainline service, and their day-in-and-day-out reliability could not be dismissed. However, the initial cost of diesels continued to frighten most railroad managements, and the diesel's sharp drop in efficiency as speed increased also kept it at "rail-length" from many properties. Why bother with a locomotive that couldn't even haul freight or be overloaded! The diesel was a racehorse, but certainly no drayhorse.

In November, 1939, out of the erection shop doors of Electro-Motive rolled a new locomotive, known by its shop order number as the 103. This locomotive consisted of four short units (each unit under fifty feet) of 1350 horsepower, for a total of 5400 horsepower. Its sleek outer shell was painted dark green with bold yellow stripes, and, unlike passenger diesels, it had a stout "bull-dog" nose and four axles per unit instead of six. More weight was concentrated on fewer axles and more traction motors—one for every axle—gave the 103 its muscle. The designers and engineers were cautious, made no claims, but invited railroads to try it out.

During the next eleven months, that 103 crisscrossed the length and breadth of this country, rolling up 83,764 miles of tonnage over 20 railroads in 35 states: through the Hoosac (no need this time to change to electrics), up Terra Alta, across Illinois, over Tennessee Pass, and out along the desert. All new and last frontiers had been crossed; the 103 had proved its worth. A true freight-hauling diesel was ready for any steam challenge. The 103 was rugged, dependable and sleek, needing no ash pits, coaling docks, roundhouses, or water plugs. Yes, the newest era in American railroading had begun. Orders for identical diesels were placed initially by the Santa Fe, Southern, Great Northern, Western Pacific, and Denver and Rio Grande.

After the war, the steam-believers wavered, Alco and Baldwin finally tossing in the towel on steam production. Lima, traditionally the proponent of modern "Super Power" steam locomotives, found itself with only 36 steamers on order in 1948, and 31 on the books for 1949. Incredibly, the last commercially built steam locomotive in the United States, a 2-8-4 Berkshire 779, left Lima's vast halls on May 13, 1949. An era had finally ended.

From now on, talk among railroad men of 2-8-8-4's and 4-6-6-4's would be replaced by talk of B-B's and C-C's, and the "look alike" diesels would take on almost every shape imaginable. Horsepower and style would out-shout any diehards who still disdained the diesels' gaudy "paint-can potpourri!"

4016
ILLINOIS CENTRAL

Rock Island

B&O

General Motors' Electro Motive Division introduced its elegant "E" series diesel locomotives in 1938 and continued production runs of E-3s, E-4s, E-5s and E-6s until ordered to cease in 1942 by the War Production Board. All these engines had the 2,000 h.p. 2-cycle 567 engine. A notable exception, and one of my boyhood favorites, was Rock Island's fleet of "mini" 1200 h.p. TA units designed for the smart, colorful *Rocket* streamliners in 1937 *(upper left)*. My first glimpse of one of these 1200 h.p. crimson, maroon and silver *Rockets* was an indelible introduction to the diesel era. At the lower left, is diesel pacesetter B&O's blue, black, grey and gold *Royal Blue;* upper right, a Santa Fe E-3 completes her first revenue run on the *Kansas Cityan* arriving in Kansas City Union Station in April 1939. Below, two E-3s of the Chicago and North Western are allowed one hour for layover and servicing in Minneapolis, before dashing back to Chicago. These 4000 h.p. teams were given the tough assignment of handling ten lightweight cars on the 841-mile daily roundtrip between Chicago and St. Paul with six regular stops and at an average speed of 63.3 m.p.h.—statistics that other railroad managements were watching.

With weathered facades of old buildings for a backdrop, the sharp-slanted nose of Louisville and Nashville's E-6 No.770 pulls across cobblestone back streets of New Orleans. Below, Dick Kindig caught the extra move of a 42-car Rio Grande freight behind the drawbar of EMD's barnstorming, freight-seeking 103. (Notably absent are the pillars of smoke from toiling steam locomotives). The dynamometer car directly behind the locomotive monitors the diesel's performance and maintains constant phone contact with the test engineers up in the cab. This April 28, 1940 demonstration was obviously a success: G.N.'s management immediately placed an order for 48 units. To the upper left, the crew on the 103 get a quick look from the rocking cab at what they hope eventually to replace on the Santa Fe.

NASHVILLE
MUNDET CORK CORPORATION
770
770
L&N

The salesman sold! Veteran rail photographer Harley Kelso made this striking shot of new dark blue, yellow, vermilion and bronze 5400 h.p. F-Ts on the Santa Fe. When the first of 320 units began to arrive on the property, the Santa Fe already had 23 passenger diesels and 43 diesel switchers in service—more than anyone else. Below, the muffled hammering of V-16s and exhausting of steam create a resounding discord as F-Ts and steam team up on Cajon's 2.2% with the *Chief.* At right, where angels feared to tread, a quartet of new F-Ts whine downgrade past a 1931 class M-137 Baldwin 2-8-8-2 on Western Pacific's Feather River Canyon route.

908
908
WESTERN
PACIFIC

4208
2719

The F-T obviously found its market, and by year's end 1945, a total of 1095 units were built. From then on, the tide was turned. Thoreau, who knew and loved New England, talked of its beaches as "made and unmade in a day by the sea shifting its sands." I get much the same feeling when I look at the three Boston & Maine veterans drearily slumbering in silence, as the maroon and gold F-Ts that replaced them, drone by. This scene by Phil Hastings conveys the deepest meaning, to me, of any in the book.

Alco eyed the F-T and had some of its own ideas on freight diesels, but the War Production Board restricted production to the EMD F-T. Alco obtained permission to construct one three-unit diesel as a testing bed for a new 1500 h.p. engine. Known as the "Black Maria," one is shown *(upper right)* leaving Canaan, Conn. on New Haven's *Berkshire Express*. Little is known about the life of these diesels.

At War's end, Alco introduced the DL-109—their challenge to EMD's previously exclusive right to build passenger diesels under wartime restrictions. The DL-109's shell was very similar to EMD. Both diesels were riding on AIA-AIA (power-idler-power) trucks, and developed 2000 h.p. per double-engined unit. Below right, one of four Rock Island DL-109s approaches Chicago with the *Peoria Rocket*. The "Rock" took delivery of the first DL-109s in 1940, before Alco was barred from the market.

A Gulf Mobile & Ohio engineer watches signals and carefully backs his DL-109 powered *Gulf Coast Rebel* through the maze of tracks towards the stub-end platforms of St. Louis Union Station. In the foreground, one of Missouri Pacific's smart new *Eagles* departs, while Terminal switchers and a Wabash Hudson wait in the clear.

The New Haven realized that most of its steamers needed replacement and asked Alco if a single diesel could be built to handle freight at night and passengers in the daytime. The answer was the DL-109; with their larger freight-sized traction motors, they demonstrated an amazing ability to work dual-service around the clock. Above right, sporting green, orange and silver pin striping, single Dl-109 No.0773 whips past North Haven Cabin with a westbound express from Springfield; below, the westbound *Yankee Clipper* passes beneath the catenary at Mill River Tower, a minute out of the New Haven station.

NEW HAVEN

The new diesels are crippled and today the God of High Iron reigns as a super MT-75 class 4-8-2 pinch-hits in the snow, keeping the *Missouri River Eagle* "on the advertised." The 5327 was completely rebuilt in 1939, given roller bearings on every axle, Baldwin disk drivers, and a solid sheet steel drop-coupler pilot. The hogger has a powerhouse at his command and wastes no time getting out of California, Mo.

5327
5327
5327

The Missouri Pacific at first met the streamlined diesel-powered competition with standard, high-speed trains pulled by a stable of modernized steamers. But when management turned to ACF for new cars, it also placed orders with EMD for diesels with matching trim. A local freight is in the hole near Sandy Hook, Mo. and the rear brakeman takes a good look at one of the company's brand-new E's on the *Missouri River Eagle*—a passing blur of cerulean blue and white.

In 1940, three diesel-powered luxury trains were operating in each direction between Chicago and Denver. The U.P.'s *City of Denver* and Burlington's *Denver Zephyr* were the well-publicized glamour trains, with the *Rocky Mountain Rocket* more or less the orphan. My personal favorite, Rock Island's handsome maroon, crimson and silver *Rocky Mountain Rocket* opens it up through Morris, Ill. on its westbound dash. It is June, 1940 and E-6 No.629 has been on the roster just long enough to acquire a coat of road dust.

4007
F

Right after the war, Electro-Motive went to work to improve upon the E-6 and offered a new 2000 h.p. E-7 model with many internal improvements. Externally, the E-7 featured a shorter "bulldog" nose. At the left is a close-up look at the beautiful lines of E-7 No.4007, which was assigned to the Illinois Central's *Panama Limited.*

One of EMD's best customers, the Burlington, already possessed enough E units in 1950 to assign an E-7 to a commuter run *(above right).* Elderly class R-5A 2-6-2 No.2052 passes eastward through Downer's Grove, Ill. Below, Missouri Pacific's *Sunshine Special* departs St. Louis behind E-7s with the usual porthole side panels. In a matter of months, that Wabash 4-6-4 will be nosed aside by new E-7s with the 567A series V-12 engines.

By the end of 1945, EMD had over 1200 FT's on various railroad properties. Alco rushed to complete its V-12 powered 1500 h.p. FA diesel freighter and received the first order from friend Gulf Mobile and Ohio. The Alco was beautifully distinctive and classically simple in design. Above, an A-B-B-A set of FA's get the tonnage underway out of Allentown, Pa. for owner Lehigh Valley; to the right, the story is summed up in one word—CONFRONTATION! At left, a stable of lovely Alco's in the Erie's Hornell, N.Y. roundhouse where, not so long ago, men worked on the road's celebrated 2-8-4s. In my opinion, Erie did the nicest job of following the Alco cab diesel's forms with their yellow paint trim over black.

725
GM&O
727
GM&O
701
GM&O

523
FRISCO

Many railroads used one paint scheme for their passenger diesels and another for freight. The Frisco's passenger diesels were a dazzling scarlet and gold, while their freight units featured a more prosaic black and yellow. At the upper left, two Frisco FAs have a good roll southward out of Kansas City with 90 cars.

New York Central, traditionally faithful to Alco, had the most 1500 h.p. diesels. To a photographer, the ideal lashup (multiple unit combination) is a set with an A, or cab unit, on each end. Herb Harwood caught the ultimate in diesel lashups *(upper left)*—Alco FAs in A-B-B-B-B-A order, working northbound mixed freight through Darrowville, Ohio in July 1960. The Alcos had guts, but suffered from weak-crankshafts and poor oil consumption.

Below, photographer Jim Gallagher made this nighttime portrait of Alco and EMD smartly-styled competitors, side by side in their handsome Baltimore & Ohio livery.

EMD competed with Alco's F-A with its 1500 h.p. V-16 F-3. It looked essentially like the F-T, but was available in both passenger and freight gearing. Between 1946 and 1949, a total of 1,573 A&B F-3's were sold. Above and below, third No.257 climbs the 1.8% Medbury Hill near Reverse, Idaho with F-3s on the point and two of U.P's venerable 2-8-8-0s shoving on the rear. At the right, it seems obvious that the Gulf Mobile & Ohio liked F-3s! Like bees on a hive, F-3s arrive in Bloomington, Ill. off the road, while others are readied for their assignments. During steam days, this location boasted sprawling facilities where now a simple sand and oil facility stand.

GM&O
GM&O

Baldwin seemed to ignore the diesel's adaptation to mass production and made the disastrous choice of building custom-designed road units for a handful of interested railroads. Notable single-order examples *(clockwise from top left)* are: Pennsy's 48-wheel "centipede;" AIA-AIA passenger shark noses; Jersey Central's 2000 h.p. double-enders; and New York Central's (and Seaboard's) "babyface" cabs. All are gone now, but the owners never regretted having them on the roster.

Pennsy and Jersey Central were Baldwin's best diesel customers. The CNJ owned 15 "babyface" 1500 h.p. DR4-4-15s of a total of thirty-three produced. A trio of these veterans grumbles across the long Newark Bay draw with empty B&O hoppers for interchange at Allentown. Height-loving photographer, Bob Malinoski incurred the wrath of an operator as he perched precariously on a signal bridge to catch this one.

8
LVAUKEE ROAD
Olympian Hiawatha

Probably the fanciest diesels ever produced were the Fairbanks-Morse three-unit 6000 h.p. Erie-built units for Milwaukee's *Olympian Hiawatha* which entered service on June 29, 1947. Their primary color was orange, with brown trucks (and pilot stripe), maroon band, grey roof and nose-top, and with gleaming chrome trim and lettering. At the left, Jim LaVake made this portrait of the chrome-faced diesel in Minneapolis, a month after she arrived on the property.

By far the best and most popular Baldwin road diesel was the DR-4-4-15 sharknose; its unique contours attracted many camera-ready diesel fans. Pennsy's A-B-A set of sharks make up a handsome team, roaring down NKP trackage through Athol Springs, N.Y. with WB tonnage on October 11, 1952.

The first sharks were produced in 1949 and the initial A-B-B-A order went to Elgin, Joliet and Eastern. B&O, NYC and Pennsy split up the balance of orders. Its standard 608SC, eight cylinder turbo-charged diesel produced 1500 h.p. (later orders were boosted to 1600 h.p.) and helped give the engine its reputation as a rugged hauler. Below are three of the chisel-nosed engines belonging to the New York Central.

The Alco PA—most beautiful diesel ever produced. American Locomotive had to break the ice and attract some of EMD's high-speed diesel passenger market. A new identity was needed to enhance the product. Publicity played a role, but the instant appeal of the classic, straight-forward, no-nonsense lines of the PA gained it immediate acceptance. At upper left, Santa Fe's famed No. 51 gets a scrub-down at the Redondo Jct. (Los Angeles) roundhouse prior to display in Exposition Park in October, 1946. Alco customer New Haven continued their DL-109 program and ordered 27 PA-1s. The handsome *Merchant's Limited* rolls off the Connecticut River Bridge at Old Saybrook behind Hunter green and yellow Alcos. At left, the inspector removes the blue flag at Houston Union Station, and soon the straw-hatted hogger will get the highball. The train is Missouri Pacific's *Texas Eagle* to St. Louis.

New York
New Haven
and Hartford
0770
NEW HAVEN

ERIE
850

On September 24, 1946, Dad and I were on hand at the Waldorf-Astoria to hear Fred G. Gurley, President of the Santa Fe, deliver an address on "Modern Transportation." After dinner and a program of Apache, Jemez and Zuni tribal dances, we all took elevators down to a Grand Central track to look at what we were honoring—American Locomotive Company's 75,000th locomotive, the resplendent 6000 h.p. diesel electric No.51 *(pictured on the preceding page)*. No one dreamed that this steam replacement would, over the next twenty years, endear itself to rail fans everywhere—and earn the distinction of being called "honorary steam locomotive!"

I call the picture at left "competitors behind paint." It was taken at Binghamton, N.Y. of rival Erie and Lehigh Valley PAs. On this page, two unlikely combinations: three elegant PAs on a Pennsy ore train northbound between Flint and Lewis Center, Ohio, and a lashup of PA and FB's roaring out of Victorville, California with a Los Angeles-bound extra, filled with Boy Scouts heading to their Jamboree. The "D-5" taped on the PAs flank was Union Pacific's way of identifying special trains. No matter what the assignment, the PAs lent real class to the head end.

The PA is handsome no matter what color you paint it! Three of my favorites are MoP's, Santa Fe's and Nickel Plate's. To the left, the 8002 and 8003 make time with the *River Eagle* east of Sedalia, Mo. under a storm-threatening sky, while *(upper right)*, the *Grand Canyon* comes out of an early Spring downpour and flushes an Osprey from her nest east of Riverside, Cal. Below right, the conductor chats with the head end crew of Nickel Plate's *New Yorker* minutes before departure time out of Chicago's La Salle Street Station.

The railroad that started it, ended it. Santa Fe, which ordered the original prototype trio was operating the last PAs on Nos.23 and 24, the *Grand Canyon* in 1967-1968. Perhaps more fans rushed to trackside than ever before to pay last respects to a great locomotive. Above, in the last few moments of sunlight, big Alcos No.67 and 75 coil the *Grand Canyon* up through Cajon eastward toward Chicago on December 24, 1968—perhaps their last day. On the opposite page, a good look at flat-faced No.70, idling in Los Angeles Terminal—their *biblika-biblika* chant soon to be gone forever.

70
SANTA FE

In deepest Indiana, an old wooden bridge, giant Elm and Monon's train No.5 make up the perfect ingredients for a late Indian summer afternoon *(above left)*. The Louisville-bound *Thoroughbred* climbs up out of Greencastle, Ind. behind its single F-7 in October, 1957.

EMD produced more F-7s than any other diesel —close to 4000! The F-7 came with high capacity electrical equipment, giving it greater tonnage ratings than the "look-alike" F-3. It was also available in four-foot longer passenger models equipped with steam heating facilities. Two roads which relied heavily on the F-7 were *(bottom left)* Chicago and Great Western, and *(opposite)* Western Pacific. The CGW often lashed-up as many as eight units on their symbols, while Western Pacific entrusted their cruise train, the *California Zephyr,* to F-7s.

There is an awesome beauty to the sheer size of railroads. And yet as you stand back and look up at the towering Tinker's Creek Viaduct, all normal perspective is lost. Three toy-like New York Central F-7s rumble across the viaduct south of Cleveland with a solid train of N&W coal-laden hoppers headed for the docks at Lake Erie. Credit Herb Harwood for this powerful picture *(following pages)*.

Two traditions in New England were broken when a diesel locomotive showed up under the Boston & Albany's Beacon Park coal pocket and it had come from a new diesel builder. It was a three-unit 6000 h.p. Fairbanks-Morse C-Liner shown at left in 1950, waiting in the shadow of the coaling dock for its next assignment west over the Berkshires. These FMs packed opposed-piston ten-cylinder engines patterned after the company's long history of marine engines. The OP had two crankshafts turning a single generator and produced tremendous power in less space.

EMD's final passenger cab unit production line was the 2250 h.p. E-8, powered by two 1125 h.p. 567B V-12s. Four hundred fifty nine of these long port-holed diesels were produced, not including older Es that were re-built for many of the railroads. In 1954, a 2400 h.p. version with a 567C engine was offered but no external changes from the E-8 were made. EMD dubbed this more powerful model the E-9, and after building ninety-nine units, ceased all passenger cab production—the end of a glorious line of champions. At the upper left, the head end crew of Southern's E-8 powered *Crescent Limited* waits for the highball north out of Birmingham; and below, the same ceremony takes place with two Milwaukee E-9 powered commuter trains out of Chicago. The picture was made before Riverside Plaza covered over the platform ends at Union Station.

5015
5015
NEW YORK
CENTRAL
SYSTEM

21

CHICAGO GREAT WESTERN

In praise of pioneers! Without fanfare, these are some of the engines that inspired the diesel-dream. Before *Zephyr,* were the doodlebugs, gas-electrics, distellates, puddle-jumpers, railcars, motors, or what-have-you. Pictured *(clockwise, from top left)* are some of the breed that survived into the Fifties: Washington & Old Dominion Railroad's car No. 5 unloading mail at Vienna, Va. in March, 1951; B&O's Ingersoll-Rand powered No.195, originally No.1 and now at St. Louis Museum of Transport; and Rock Island's No.9011 leaving St. Louis with a local in February, 1951. This unit was originally a gas-electric, later converted to a Caterpillar diesel.

Without them, the trains couldn't run. It would be impossible to cover, even in part, the vital story of the work-a-day diesel switchers that made a big—but little-noticed—impact upon this nation's railroads. On the preceding page is my personal tribute to the crews, and that all-important aspect of behind-the-scenes railroading that receives so little attention.

GULF MOBILE & OHIO
GULF MOBILE & OHIO
Rock Island

PIER - 66
195

These silent sentinels of bygone days bear mute, yet eloquent, testimony to the final surrender of steam. Even today, at trackside, many of these haunting relics dot the American scene—a nostalgic reminder of the golden days of steam.

CHICAGO
AND
NORTHWEST
RAILWAY

Coming events cast their shadows before them

6

In 1951, I started satisfactorily documenting my railroad experiences (and feelings) with good cameras. That year also saw the beginning of an important new era of dieselization for the railroads—that of the introduction of the "ugly" general purpose "hood unit" diesel which finally drove the once-proud steamers out to pasture. Ironically, the hood unit would eventually also displace the earlier streamlined diesels.

The introduction of the general purpose hood units was not heralded by the fanfare for which earlier diesels are remembered. Instead, the "geep" (as this new breed was called) was billed as an all-purpose unit. Simple in design, it was easily adaptable to branch-line service, drag, and—"if necessary"—passenger service. It was bi-directional and was designed with nothing more than an all-accessible shell for easy maintenance. What more could a railroad ask! Between late 1949 and 1954, seventy-four railroads purchased "geeps." Any individuality that these hood units could possibly engender came out of a paint can (but the operating statistics and cost sheet economics did not include the cost of the paint)!

As more and more railroads dieselized, tracking down the last strongholds of steam became increasingly difficult for those of us searching for them. As winter approached, we'd hear of another railroad dropping the last of its fires; and come summer, we would look hopefully for a possible resurgence of traffic that *just might* necessitate bringing steam out of storage.

I'll never forget one late night in 1957 when I drove up to the outer yard limits of the huge Norfolk and Western complex at Roanoke, Virginia. Several tracks over, in the dark of the outer yard, I could see the dim outlines of a long train of loaded hopper cars and hear the endlessly repeating *bang-bang, bang-bang* as they rattled through a cross-over and out onto the main. The pulse of the train picked up, and slack slammed past and back through the moving hoppers. The dark train kept passing along into the night, out towards the mountains and Blue Ridge. Down toward the yard and its high floodlights, a billowing, silvery-white, tumbling plume of steam approached. Within seconds the dimly lit caboose passed, with a huge clanking, hissing Y-6 mallet shoving on the rear, the marvelous *ka-dunk, ka-donk, ka-dunk, ka-donk* noise of its pounding rods, the sharp hammering exhaust, all blending into the drum-roll thunder of the going train. Surely, everyone within miles would awaken, but this was the life of Roanoke and the Norfolk and Western. Position light signals winked their eerie yellow patterns after the eastbound train.

From the east, over towards the mountains, a dull rumbling cadence could be heard. A single chilling "hoot" whistle echoed through the cool night air and you waited and listened. The rumbling increased, and within minutes the dark rails came alive with an inbound train. Two monstrously proportioned articulateds held down the helm, shaking the ground as they passed. The lead engine's headlight picked out its way down into the yard, and again I was watching what seemed to be an endless train of empty black hoppers coming in from the east: *bang-bang, bang-bang; bang-bang, bang-bang.* The slowing train fanned up a breeze of coal smoke, steam, and hot metal brake shoes as it rumbled past and finally came to a squealing halt down in the yard.

An 0-8-0 switcher quietly chuffed into view, down by the rear end of the train—the whine of its turbogenerator clearly heard. A lantern signaled in circles from the front of the locomotive, and somewhere in the dark came the reply. The 0-8-0 chuffed back, past the hoppers and out of sight, leaving lonely white whisps of steam.

Down at the Shaffers Crossing engine terminal, I later discovered that the two Roanoke-built giants that had come in from the east were only a few years old. In just one hour, both were readied for their next assignments east! Shaffers Crossing was an incredibly busy and efficient place, used to servicing well over 100 engines in a shift with the most modern facilities available. Incidentally, a copy of the wheel report from the yard office showed that the tonnage on that last outbound job exceeded 10,000 tons! Unheard of elsewhere—routine for the N & W. Surely steam would always be *here*!

Little did I realize, that steam-filled night, that in three short years, I would be journeying to Louisville to ride on a L&N special behind the only steam locomotive they could find: a borrowed Illinois Central 4-8-2. Equally unimaginable was the fact that Nickel Plate's celebrated Berkshires were no longer running, nor had there been a steamer out of Kansas City since May of '55.

In the early 1960's, when the seemingly unreal was finally accepted, we scurried to the backwoods to relive the golden age of steam in miniature, falling in love with roads like the Buffalo Creek and Gauley, Georgia Pacific, Magma Arizona, and Mobile and Gulf. This too, all came to an end—as total and swift as that of the Norfolk and Western's great steam world. Another book and another time will be needed to cover the final glorious moments of the last big steam strongholds—chasing an incredible lash-up of three big B&O EM-1's on coal that ended up with a pulled drawbar; riding across Nebraska in the cab of a Union Pacific 4-8-4 just out of storage, and making better time, with more refers, and more crosswinds, than the diesels that day; riding in the *Ohio State Limited's* dining car and watching two Nickel Plate "Berks" pounding along next to us on a parallel track with a westbound time freight—and at the same speed!

The many great silent electric locomotives, and the powerful second generation diesels that now head this nation's trains, will have to wait. So too the shortlines, the last cab-diesels, the fan trips, and the tourist pikes—all will have to come at a later time. What follows is a brief look at electric railroading, steam shortlines and second generation diesels.

In the market of diesel road switchers, Alco got the jump on EMD after the war with its RS series hood units. Well over four hundred RS-2s were sold between 1946 and 1950, followed by over 1500 RS-3s. Alco had a good thing going for itself. In 1948, EMD countered with the "odd-ball" BL-1, called the Branch Line. Nine roads bought a total of 58 production models cataloged as BL-2. EMD had clearly missed out. At extreme right top, two of Monon's nine BL-2s team up with an F-7 cab for road service; below, two of Alco's round-nosed RS classics assist a big Delaware & Hudson Alco-built K-62 class 4-8-4. The Alco diesels obviously offered this fireman a chance to see the scenery!

In 1949, EMD's design and engineering staff decided to eliminate frills in favor of function for its new line of locomotives. They sought simplicity in servicing and design and practicality in "general purpose" operations; the resulting locomotive was a pleasingly utilitarian creature known as the GP-7. In the center, the 578 waits in the hole as sister GP-7 No.573 heads a freight out of Freeport, Maine. Maine Central's new "Pine Tree" paint scheme typifies management's faith in facelifting the "ugly darlings" from a paint can!

573
573
MAINE
The PINE TREE Route
CENTRAL

30
30

4053

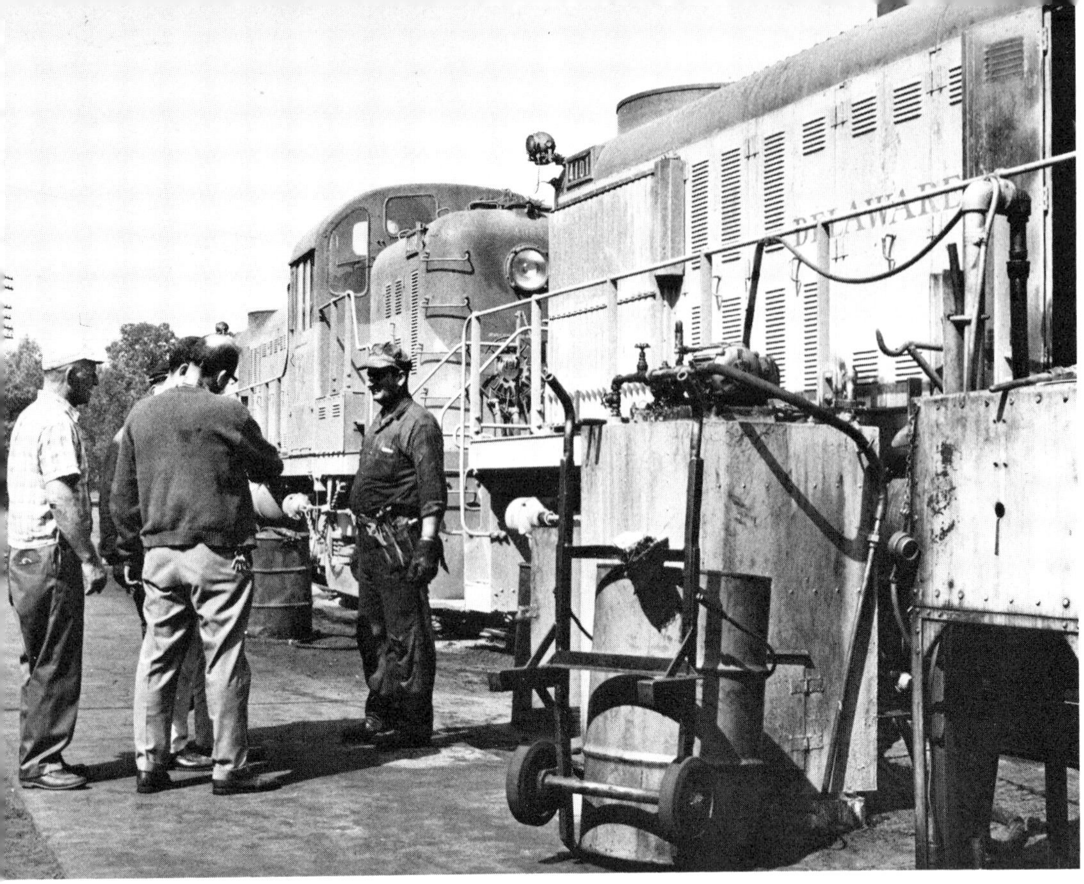

"Do it this way, fellas." RS-3 shop talk at Mechanicsville, N.Y. on the Delaware & Hudson.

Below, the quaint charm of rural America is very much in evidence as the crew of New Haven's Danbury to Lakeville local spots an empty box for the grain merchant in Canaan, Conn. Their engine is a brand new RS-3.

On the right is a scene reminiscent of steam days as Union Pacific's GP-9 No.317 takes on sand at Council Bluffs, Iowa. This is the only aspect of diesel servicing that is performed in the same manner as with steam locomotives.

NO CLEARANCE
UP
317

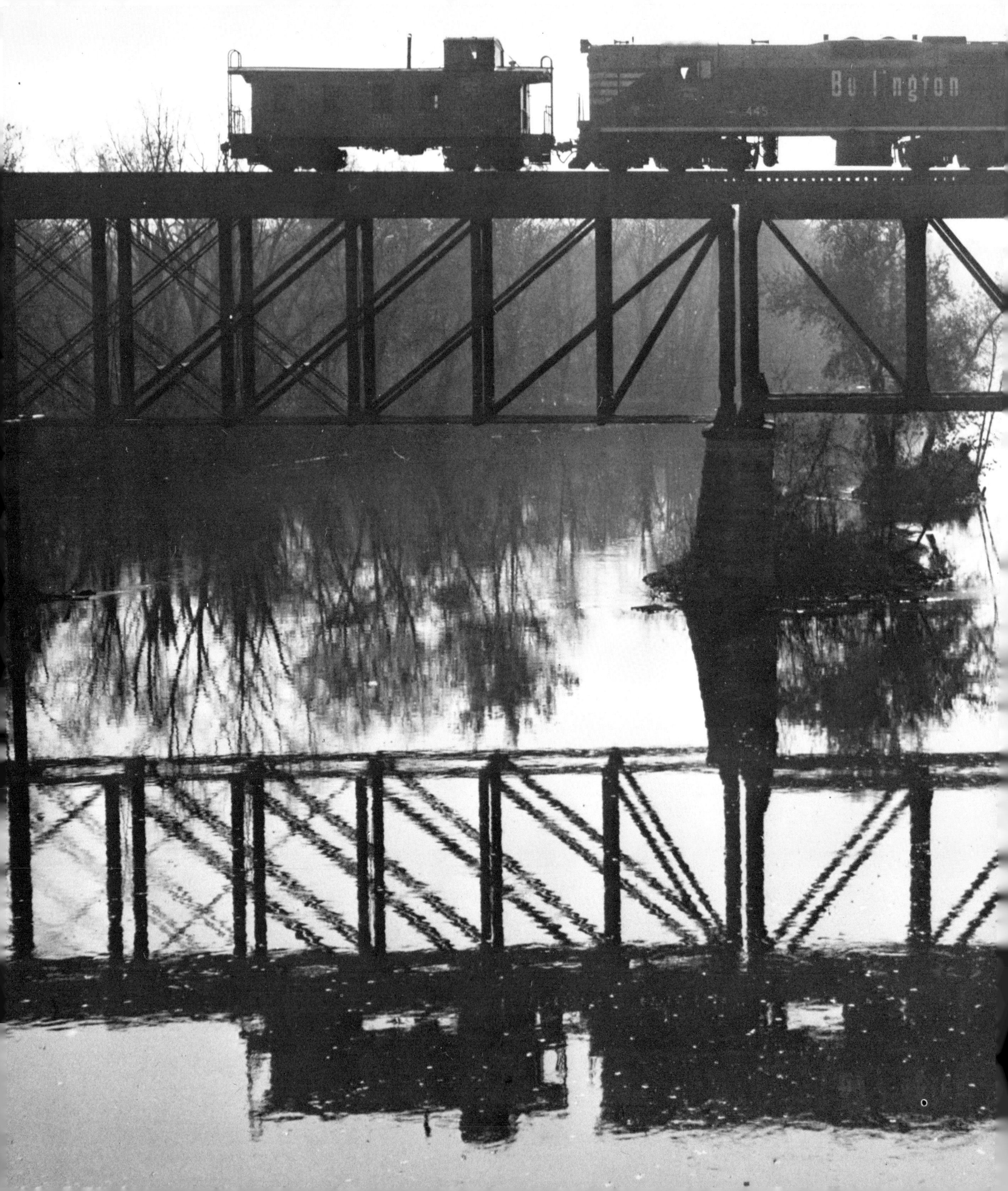
445

Looking back over the varied history of railroad operations, it is almost universally agreed that the Norfolk & Western built and employed the finest steam locomotives in the land. While most roads stabled no fewer than a half dozen wheel arrangements for freight, N&W concentrated on, and perfected, just two. The locomotives were as different as day and night, but each was faultless in performing its mission.

On the immediate right, is a single expansion 70-inch drivered articulated class A, capable of handling heavy passenger trains at 70 m.p.h. or racing 14,500 tons (200 hoppers) over level track. To the far right, Y-6 compound 2-8-8-2 No.2143 blasts out of Mattawan Tunnel, W. Va. trailing 8000 tons of coal on her drawbar. This most powerful locomotive can develop 152,206 lbs. tractive effort. N&W's efficiency was 100% thorough—from design and construction, to operating and servicing.

On the preceding page, two Burlington SD-9s slowly rumble across the misty, placid Fox River at Sheridan, Ill. enroute to Wedron. The SD-9 is an outgrowth of the geep, offering two additional power axles with Flexicoil trucks, ideally spreading its weight for light-rail, heavy tonnage service.

DO NOT WALK
NOR TRESPASS ON
THE BRIDGE

A Blue Ridge symphony of steel, steam and thunder is performed at sunrise by the eastbound passage of one of Norfolk and Western's gigantic coal trains. The road engine is class A No.1237, and the helper on the point is Y-6 No.2150; on the rear, Y-6 No.2158—all three contributing a total of 418,412 lbs. of massive tractive effort!

By the time the hack passes, the sun has risen higher and the shadows are noticeably shorter. No.2158's injector and tender water-warmer leaves a wake of condensing steam. A spectacular display of steam was provided by the N&W after diesels had moved into the roundhouses of the other railroads. Some of my fondest memories are of the roaring cadence of an A, and the furious exhaust of a Y working in tandem up Blue Ridge.

In 1956, when divisions under steam could be counted on fingers, the Pennsy had two freight strongholds still dominated by steam. Places like Mt. Carmel, Shamokin, Carrothers and Attica Jct. became shrines for rail fans who converged from all 48 states. In the autumn of their careers, two of Pennsy's "Big Hippo" Decapods knuckle down to the torturous task of moving ninety cars of ore up the 1.3% grade from Shamokin to Mt. Carmel, Pa. Two more of these 2-10-0 brutes are shoving on the rear.

When the War Production Board clamped down on Pennsy's locomotive design efforts, the road quickly settled for 125 home-built 2-10-4s from C&O blueprints. The result was a fabulous machine that out-lasted many diesels. J-1 No.6421 skirts a tornado and is about to storm over the B&O's iron at Attica Jct., Ohio—the Columbus-bound empties will bang away at the crossover with a shaking, rhythmic cadence. The view is from the tower that became a favorite vantage point for steam-starved photographers in the mid-fifties.

How I loved the B&O back in the summers of 1956 and 1957! A phone call to John Sell, Superintendent in Wheeling, would usually result in my hopping in the car and heading straight for Benwood Jct. "The 5308 was on 43 today—we've got several 7600s on call—the 4534..." That was all I needed to get out of New York, and it gave me plenty to think about on the drive.

My favorite B&O locomotive was their largest—the 2-8-8-4 EM-1. They were beautiful (like all B&O locomotives) and they were big. Their fire-boxes were 25 feet long with a grate measuring 14′9″ by 8′; and an inside height to the crown sheet of 6′3″, enough room to hold a dinner party for twelve people! Their last assignments were coal drags, and the roundhouses at Benwood (Wheeling), Holloway and Lorain were teeming with them! Probably the most spectacular show of EM-1s ever staged was in September 1956 when the 7625, 7603 and 7611 attacked Swine Creek Hill with a De Forest-to-Painesville coal train—their six-stacked havoc shaking heaven and earth. On the right, a portrait of the 7621 under a storm-threatening sky.

670
B&O

View from the right-hand cushion. A steamy August rain squall pours down from the skies, drenching everything in and around McMechen, W. Va. It is 1957 and all the steam locomotives have been renumbered into three digits while diesels retain the four digit numbers. We're holding the main in the 650 (last year's 7600) while the 670 (originally the 7619) pulls down the south siding. The year before, both engines were cherished friends, but with their new numbers, something was missing. Maybe it was my certainty of their survival.

Below, at Willard, two more renumbered friends stand on the ready track in September, 1957. The "Big Six" 2-10-2 No.531 is the original 1926 Baldwin-built S-1a No.6200. The 716 is the ex-5574, a homebuilt T-3 class 4-8-2 built in 1944. Both are nearing the end of their careers and B&O;s loving care is still very evident.

The Nickel Plate never knew what "competition" meant once it received its 125 incomparable Berkshires. These engines went to work to earn the NKP kudos as "the route of high-speed service." With a wide-open throttle, No.707 rolls grandly across Ohio under her canopy of steam in 1957 *(at right)*. In a year, management would reluctantly announce their "temporary withdrawal from service," as the diesels started to arrive. Sister 777 gets eastbound IB-64 out of Conneaut, Ohio.

707

There is a satisfying sense of fulfillment in seeing a steam locomotive down on her hands and knees, so to speak, working every inch of the way, battling beneath her pillar of smoke, blasting ever upwards. Bob Malinoski waited for hours in a windswept canyon of Sherman Hill to make the photograph of Union Pacific's Big Boy No.4014 *(above)*, the largest in the world, sweating up Sherman with westbound freight. His time was well spent. Other celebrities left in U.P.'s stable at the very end of steam were the 100 m.p.h. 4-8-4s *(above, right)* and the 4-6-6-4 Challengers; one of which is seen *(below, right)* with a 4-8-8-4. Unlike most other railroads, Union Pacific kept its finest steam in mainline service until the end.

UNION PACIFIC
832

UNION PACIFIC

2511

A sentinel tree bears mute witness to the stormy passage of Burlington's handsome M-4 No.6312 lugging southern Illinois coal into the twilight *(above)*. While other railroads were ordering big Northerns, Challengers and the like, the Illinois Central concentrated on on rebuilding 1920 vintage 2-10-2s into 70-inch drivered 4-8-2s that boasted more tractive effort than most Northerns, and modernizing 2-10-2s into super "Centrals" that could lug 10,000 tons on level ground. A "souped-up" Paducah (Ky.) shop 4-8-2 tromps through Central City, Ill. *(left)*, with a mainline train south, in the summer of 1955.

3642
3642
2819
2819

When the passing of big steam became fact, we crossed the Canadian border and made new acquaintances on the CPR and CNR. From the wine-red livery of Canadian Pacific, and the green and gold of Canadian National came many colorful locomotives that we fell in love with. For a change of pace, these pages depict some of the more prosaic power that captured my interest. To the left, an elderly Canadian Pacific class N2a 2-8-0 pulls past handsome H1b 4-6-4 No.2819 at St. Luc, Ont., while *(above, right)* a Canadian National S1f 2-8-2 departs Hamilton, Ont., in her mantle of cylinder cock steam. Below, a G1V 4-6-2 backs out of the Jane Street (Toronto) roundhouse onto the table.

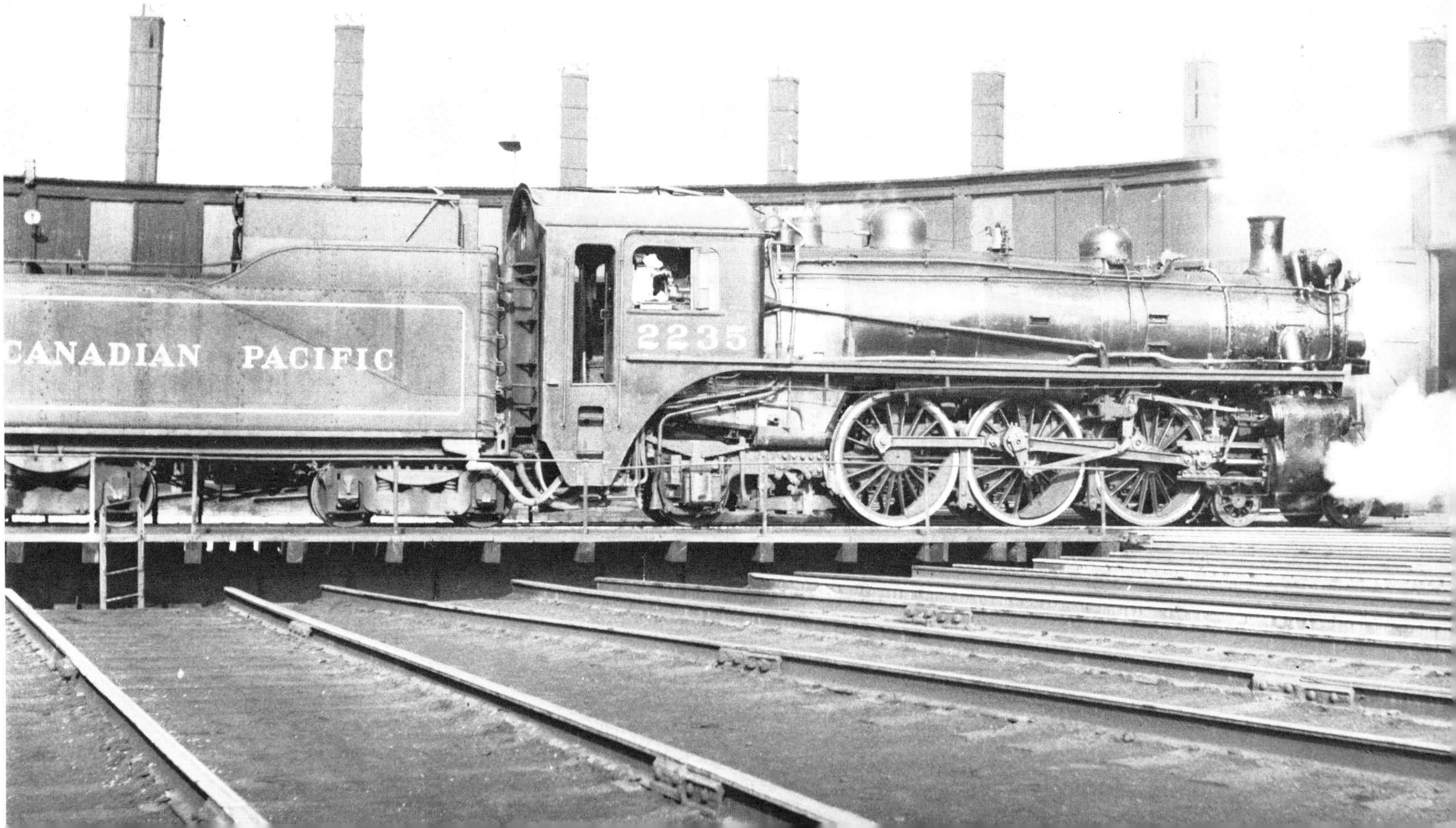

NEW HAVEN
373

357

A whole picture book could, and should, be devoted to the history of electric railroading in the United States. I have spent the greater portion of my life near the New Haven, the railroad for which Westinghouse built the first 11,000 volt, 25-cycle, single-phase A.C. system back in 1907, and have spent considerable time documenting the regrettable phasing out of electric locomotives.

Above, seen in the condition she was in just after Penn Central took over, EP-5 GE "Jet" No.373 speeds *The Hell Gate* through Stamford, Conn. Below, the favorite of the crews—an EP-3 Westinghouse "flat-bottom"—reaches for the wires and rushes through Harrison, N.Y. with the fleet *Merchant's Limited.* On the right, two EF-4 ex-Virginian ignatron rectifier freight motors wait between assignments at Cedar Hill.

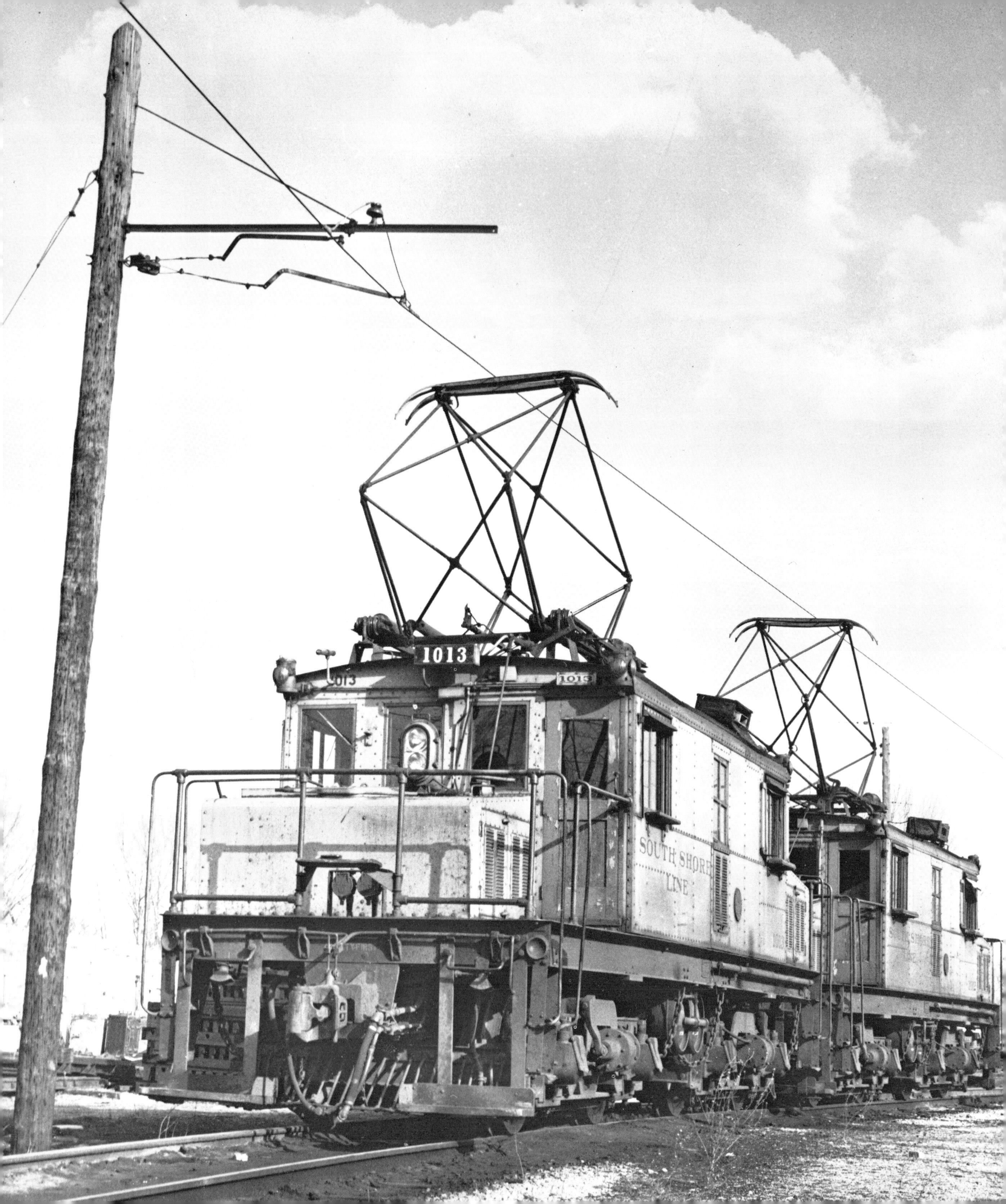

1013
1013
1013
SOUTH SHORE
LINE

A New York Central 600-volt D.C. class P-motor lays over on the yard lead at North White Plains, N.Y. This massive electric was built by G.E. in 1929 for the Cleveland Union Terminal Railroad where it operated on 3,000-volt D.C. overhead. On the left , two South Shore motors have cut off a work train and head into the Michigan City, Ind., shops. March 1964.

BLT 6·25

Everything that could possibly be said or written in praise of the legendary GG-1 has been chronicled. Built in 1934, these marvelous machines are still delivering dependable day-in, day-out passenger and freight service, in the *Broadway Limited* or tri-level auto carriers. Capable of speeds in easy excess of 100 m.p.h. and short-time output of 8,500 h.p., there has never been, *to this day,* an engine that could be compared in any way! Although they are usually pictured on the point of a high-speed passenger run, I prefer to show one of these classics digging in with three RS-3s on the Chalk Point coal train leaving Bay View, Md. To the right, two Virginian GE rectifiers hum through a cut east of Princeton, W. Va.; at left, South Shore's "Little Joe" motor No.802 switches near Ogden Dunes, Ind.

In the early sixties, when mainline steam was all but a memory, I would revel in the dampness of the dewy morning air and look at the fascinating rust patterns on the rails—soon to be polished by a chunky Buffalo Creek & Gauley 2-8-0, working empties up to the Widen Tipple.

Above right, on a cold February morning, the track gang warms up around a fire as stout No.97, Mobile & Gulf's sole locomotive, wheezes off to Brownsville under what purports to be a full head of steam. This was the last freight-only common carrier behind steam. Friend, Mike Koch, aptly called the Shays "titans of the timber." In the early 1960s these geared locomotives were still working in the deep woods and at the saw mills. Long before their twilight, Andy Wittenborn frequented the back hills in search of the picturesque creek-forging, hill-climbing Shay. A favorite—Georgia Pacific's No.19 grinds out of the woods, heading towards Swandale, W. Va.

The light rails of the Magma Arizona Railroad wandered through the empty desert from Magma Jct. up to Superior, a copper town at the base of the Superstitions. The "up-train" brushes her cylinders with the sage at ties' end, approaching a crossing that hardly warrants identification, let alone the warning.

The Shay looked like she belonged back in the woods somewhere —out of sight; and in most cases Shays did just that, where rail was uncertain. Twin Seam's balloon-stacked No.8 embellishes her surroundings with a grand cover of soot, near Kellerman, Ala. Artist Phil Ronfor, a lover of geared locomotives, captured the mood.

867
S.P.&S.
RY
HYDRANT
150
150

During the evolution of the diesel it was inevitable that increasingly more powerful units would be developed. In 1960, EMD introduced the low-nosed 2000 h.p. GP-20, and initiated their now well-known locomotive trade-in program. At the upper left, three Santa Fe GP-20s do the work of four former F-units, lifting a westbound hotshot up from the Mississippi River bottoms and Ft. Madison, Iowa. Below , the evolution of the diesel is graphically portrayed in the Spokane, Portland and Seattle Railway's Vancouver, Wash., yards.

With the success of EMD's trade-in program, the generic-term, "second generation" diesel emerged, referring to the new replacements. A "14-L" is loudly chimed as a lashup of Lehigh & Hudson River's Alco Century 420s and an RS-3 moves Maybrook-bound tonnage into Warwick, N.Y., with a vengeance! It is February, but the plow-equipped No.22 has no snow to contend with. The ground is frozen, but the day is unseasonably warm, with temperatures in the 50s, carrying a touch of spring fever.

The pooling of power came into being with the practice of MU-ing various builder's diesels. Power pools enabled connecting railroads to run through trains without changing engines. Two Burlington GP-40s and a GE U-25 growl down the iron of the Erie-Lackawanna through Suffern, N.Y., with symbol NE-74 from Chicago and the West. Chances are, E-L power will be heading the westbound counterpart.

903
903
GM O

36
36
U.P. 36
UNION
PACIFIC

Standing in a railroad terminal or yard these days, one feels much the same as when standing near an airport apron longing to see Connies and DC-6s. Tremendous high-horsepower, jet-whining turbocharged diesel titans have taken over.

Clockwise, from upper left, twelve thousand horsepower worth of Gulf Mobile & Ohio's SD-40s knuckle down to moving the massive Commonwealth Edison unit train south out of Joliet power station towards the mine at Percy, Ill.; Santa Fe's semi-streamlined hood/cab U30CG geared for 95 m.p.h. operations; Erie-Lackawanna's 3,430 h.p. General Electric C-C U34CHs for push-pull commuter operations and weekend freight service; and Union Pacific's high and mighty 5,000 h.p. U-50 Bs moving in a triple hook-up of 15,000 h.p. These big fellows typify the best of today's super-diesels.

3642
3642
3642

We've come a long way since the 2-8-0s, 2-10-2s, F-Ts and GP-9s. Unlike steam, the guts of the diesel are always well out of sight—wedged solidly down over its wheels; but the now-familiar utilitarian shell of sheet metal has established a style that has captured the fancy of today's second generation railroader and rail fan alike. Two Erie-Lackawanna EMD SD-45s lay over in the Croxton yards to head the evening *Apollo* hotshot freight to Buffalo. The yard engine makes up the train.

LOOK OUT FOR FALLEN ROCKS
C&O

Photographic credits

Credits for all photographs are shown below by page number. When more than one photograph appears on a page, the top, or upper photo is indicated first. When two photographs taken by the same photographer appear by themselves on the same page, one credit is given. Those identified by "collection" refer to negatives in the author's collection.

Jacket (front)—Ball
Jacket (back)—E.T. Harley (U.P. —Ball)

page 1—Ball; *2*—Ball; *4-5* Ball; *6*—Ball; *8*—James P. Gallagher; *10-11* Jeffrey K. Winslow; *12*—Philip R. Hastings; *17*—Ball; *18*—Herb Harwood; *23*—Ball; *24*—Ball; *28*—T.J. Donahue; *56*—TRAINS; *92*—Andrew Wittenborn; *94*—Ball; *95*—T.J. Donahue; *166*—*Railroad Magazine*; *200*—collection; *251*—Ball.

Chapter 1

30 Kent Cochrane; *31* collection; *32* T.J. Donahue; *33* collection; *34* Bud Rothaar; *35* collection; *36* collection; *37* collection; Southern Railway; *38* collection; *39* William Barham; *40 & 41* collection; *42 & 43* collection; *44 & 45* collection; *46-47* William Barham; *48* William Barham; collection; *49* Richard Kindig; *50 & 51* Richard Kindig; *52* collection; *53* Richard Kindig; *54* Harley Kelso; *55* William Barham.

Chapter 2

58 Courtesy of Ed Nowak; *59* TRAINS; *60* Rail Photo Service; collection; *61* collection; *Railroad* Magazine; *62 & 63* Richard Kindig; *64* courtesy of Ed Nowak; *65* Richard Kindig; *66 & 67* collection; *68* *Railroad* Magazine; collection; *69* collection; *70* collection; *71* courtesy Ed Nowak; REA Express; *72 & 73* courtesy Ed Nowak; *74 & 75* courtesy Ed Nowak; *76* O. Winston Link; *77* Ball; collection; *78 & 79* print collection; *78* collection; *79* Robert Collins; *80* Ball; courtesy Ed Nowak; *81* Richard Cook; *82* Harley Kelso; *83* collection; *84-85* Stan Kistler; *86* Robert Malinoski; *87* Harley Kelso; *88* Richard Kindig; *89* collection; *90* Charles E. Winters; collection; *91* collection.

Chapter 3

96 & 97 Philip R. Hastings; *98* Ball; *99* Robert Collins; *100 & 101* collection; *102* Philip R. Hastings; *103* Jim Shaughnessy; *104 & 105* collection; *106* T.J. Donahue; *107* collection; Robert Collins; *108 & 109* Ball; *110* Ball; *111* collection; Ball; *112 & 113* Frank Schlegel; *114 & 115* Ball; *116* Ball; Robert Collins; *117* Robert Collins; *118 & 119* Robert Collins; *120* Robert Collins; *121* John Pickett; *122 & 123* Robert Collins; *124* collection; *125* Robert Collins; *126* Fletcher Swan; *127* collection; Charles E. Winters collection; *128* T.J. Donahue; *129* Ball; *130 & 131* collection; *132 & 133* T.J. Donahue; *134-135* Robert Collins; Rail Photo Service; *135* collection; *136* Ed Nowak; collection; *137* collection; Ray Buhrmaster; *138 & 139* collection; *140* collection; *141* William Barham; *142-143* Donald E. Smith; *144 & 145* Robert Olmsted; *146* Robert Olmsted; *147* Ball; *148 & 149* William Kratville; *150* collection; Richard Kindig; *151* Ball; collection; *152* Ball; *153* collection; Richard Kindig; *154* collection; Rail Photo Service; *155* Rail Photo Service; *156* Henry R. Griffiths, Jr.; *157* collection; *158* collection; *159* Henry R. Griffiths, Jr.; Philip R. Hastings; *160* Philip R. Hastings; *161* collection; Henry R. Griffiths; *162 & 163* Henry R. Griffiths, Jr.; *164* William Barham; *165* Harley Kelso.

Chapter 4

168 Andrew Wittenborn; *169* O. Wilson Link; *170* Fletcher Swan; Robert Collins; *171* Fletcher Swan; *172* Ball; *173* Andrew Wittenborn; Ball; *174* J.J. Young; Ball; *175* Ball; *176* Andrew Wittenborn (whistle); Ball; *177* Ball; *178 & 179* Philip R. Hastings; *180 & 181* all courtesy Ed Nowak, except L-4b; *182* Ed Nowak; *183* courtesy Ed Nowak; Ball; *184* Ray Buhrmaster; *185* Fletcher Swan; *186 & 187* Philip R. Hastings; *188 & 189* Ball; *190* Andrew Wittenborn; *191* Herb Harwood; *192* Andrew Wittenborn; Herb Harwood; *193* Ball; *194* Philip A. Weibler; *195* Philip R. Hastings; *196* Ball; collection; Robert Malinoski; *197* Howard Fogg; *198* Richard Steinheimer; *199* Jim Shaughnessy.

Chapter 5

202 C.&E.I.; *203* James G. LaVake; *204* collection; Ball; *205* collection; *206* Santa Fe Ry; Richard Kindig; *207* Ball; *208* Harley Kelso; William Barham; *209* collection; *210* Philip R. Hastings; *211* collection; *212* collection; *213* T.J. Donahue; *214-215* collection; *216 & 217* collection; *218* Ball; *219* Ray Buhrmaster; collection; *220* Ball; print collection; *221* GM&O; *222* Robert Olmsted; Herb Harwood; *223* James P. Gallagher; *224* Henry R. Griffiths, Jr.; *225* Ball; *226* clockwise from top right; collection; collection; Walt Grosselfinger, Jr., Ed Nowak; *227* Robert Malinoski; *228* James G. LaVake; *229* collection; courtesy Ed Nowak; *230* Fletcher Swan; Don Sims; *231* T.J. Donahue; *232* J.J. Young; *233* Don Sims; S.K. Bolton (Herb Harwood collection); *234* Ball; *235* Ball; Eric Archer; *236 & 237* Ball; *238* Ball; *239* collection; *240-241* Herb Harwood; *242* Ball; *243* collection; *244 & 245* Ball; *246* Herb Harwood; *247* collection; Herb Harwood; *248 & 249* Ball.

Chapter 6

254 & 255 Ball; *255* Ball; John Pickett; *256* Ball; collection; *257* Ball; *258-259* Robert Olmsted; *260* Philip A. Weibler; *261* Ball; *262 & 263* Robert Malinoski; *264 & 265* Ball; *266* Herb Harwood; *267* Ball; *268* Ball; *269* Philip A. Weibler; *270* Herb Harwood; *271* Ball; *272* Philip A. Weibler; *273* Ball; *274* Robert Malinoski; *275* Ball; Henry R. Griffiths, Jr.; *276 & 277* Ball; *278 & 279* Ball; *280 & 281* Ball; *282* Ball; *283* Herb Harwood; *284* Ball; *285* Ball; Andrew Wittenborn; *286* Ball; *287* Phil Ronfor; *288 & 289* Ball; *290 & 291* Ball; *292 & 293* Ball; *294 & 295* Ball.

Index

This index is alphabetically arranged by railroad with steam, diesel and electric appearing in that order. Steam locomotives are designated by railroad class and wheel arrangement, diesels by builder's model and wheel arrangement, and electric by railroad class and wheel arrangement. It should be noted that in multiple-unit diesel lash ups, the lead unit only appears in the index. In many cases, railroads did not assign class designation to their engines—in these cases, the type of locomotive is listed in parenthesis. (In many cases, the same class of locomotive appears on several pages.) Page numbers are indicated in italics.

Alton Railroad

class P-1b, 4-6-2 . . . *45*

American Locomotive

("Black Maria"), B-B . . . *211*

Atchison, Topeka & Santa Fe

class 1950, 2-8-0 . . . *185*
class 3160, 2-8-2 . . . *206*
class 3800, 2-10-2 . . . *54, 185*
class 2900, 4-8-4 . . . *147*
class 3776, 4-8-4 . . . *146, 164*
class 5011, 2-10-4 . . . *153*
#1, 1-A, (box cab), B-B . . . *60, 200*
model F-T, B-B . . . *208*
model E-1, A1A-A1A . . . *202*
model E-3, A1A-A1A . . . *205*
model PA, A1A-A1A . . . *230, 235, 236, 237*
model GP-20, B-B . . . *288*
model U30CG, C-C . . . *293*

Atlantic Coast Line

class P-5a, 4-6-2 . . . *127*
class AJ-2, 4-6-2 . . . *127*
class R-1, 4-8-4 . . . *127*
model F-3, B-B . . . *11*

Baltimore & Ohio Railroad

class P-1d, 4-6-2 . . . *128*
class P-5a, 4-6-2 . . . *170*
class P-7c, 4-6-2 . . . *172*
class P-7d, 4-6-2 . . . *88*
class V-2 ("Lord Baltimore"), 4-6-4 . . . *68*
class T-3, 4-8-2 . . . *269*
class T-4, 4-8-2 . . . *196*
class S-1a, 2-10-2 . . . *129, 269*
class EL-4, 2-8-8-0 . . . *130*
class EL-5a, 2-8-8-0 . . . *130, 131*
class EM-1, 2-8-8-4 . . . *266, 267, 268*
#195, (oil electric), B-B . . . *247*
#50 (box cab), B-B diesel . . . *60*
class EA/EB, A1A-A1A . . . *77*
model E-6, A1A-A1A . . . *204*
model F-A, B-B . . . *223*
model F-7, B-B . . . *223*

Boston & Albany

class J-2c, 4-6-4 . . . *31, 105*
class A-1, 2-8-4 . . . *31*

Boston & Maine

class B-15, 2-6-0 . . . *102*
class P-2d, 4-6-2 . . . *101*

class P-3a, 4-6-2 . . . *103*
class R-1c, 4-8-2 . . . *100*
model F-T, B-B . . . *210*

Buffalo, Creek & Gauley

class (consolidation), 2-8-0 . . . *284*

Camas Prairie Railroad

class (Mikado—U.P.), 2-8-2 . . . *161*
class (Mikado—L.A. & S.L.), 2-8-2 . . . *163*

Canadian National Railway

class S-1-f, 2-8-2 . . . *277*
class H-6-g, 4-6-0 . . . *18*
class K-5a, 4-6-4 . . . *86*
class U-1f, 4-8-2 . . . *196*

Canadian Pacific

class N2a, 2-8-0 . . . *276*
class P2f, 2-8-2 . . . *192*
class G1v, 4-6-2 . . . *277*
class H1b, 4-6-4 . . . *276*
class T-1A, 2-10-4 . . . *76*

Central Railroad of New Jersey

#1000 (oil electric), B-B . . . *56*
class T-38, 4-6-0 . . . *115*
class P-43, 4-6-2 . . . *114*
class M-63, 2-8-2 . . . *114*
model DR-6-4-20 (double-ender), A1A-A1A . . . *226*
model DR-4-4-15 ("babyface"), B-B . . . *227*

Central Vermont

class T-1b, 2-10-4 . . . *98*

Chesapeake & Ohio Railway

class L-2, 4-6-4 . . . *170, 171*
class K-4, 2-8-4 . . . *170*
class H-4, 2-6-6-2 . . . *191*
class H-8, 2-6-6-6 . . . *132, 133*

Chicago, Burlington & Quincy

class R-5a, 2-6-2 . . . *219*
class O-1a, 2-8-2 . . . *27, 44, 194*
class O-5a, 4-8-4 . . . *6,137*
class M-4a, 2-10-4 . . . *186, 187, 273*
model 9900 *(Pioneer Zephyr)* . . . *58*
9906 A/B *(Denver Zephyr)*, B-B . . . *62, 66*
9907 A/B *(Denver Zephyr)*, B-B . . . *63*
model E-5 ("Silver Speed"), A1A-A1A . . . *83*
model E-5 ("Silver Power"), A1A-A1A . . . *83*
model F-7, B-B . . . *248*
model E-7, A1A-A1A . . . *219*
model SD-9, C-C . . . *259*
model GP-40, B-B . . . *291*

Chicago & Eastern Illinois

class (Pacific), 4-6-2 . . . *43*

Chicago Great Western

class K-5, 4-6-2 . . . *142-143*
model SW-1, B-B . . . *244-245*
model F-7, B-B . . . *238*

Chicago, Milwaukee, St. Paul & Pacific

class A, 4-4-2 . . . *68*
class F-7, 4-6-4 . . . *70*
model 20A-P, A1A-A1A . . . *228*
model E-9, A1A-A1A . . . *242*

Chicago & Northwestern

class E, 4-6-2 . . . *42, 136*
class E-4, 4-6-4 . . . *70*
oil-electric B-B . . . *42*
#CD-07A, B, C *(City of Denver)*, B-B . . . *65, 67*
#LA-1,2,3, class E-2 *(City of Los Angeles)*, A1A-A1A . . . *65*
model E-3, A1A-A1A . . . *205*
model E-8, A1A-A1A . . . *249*

Chicago, Rock Island & Pacific

class M-50a, 4-8-2 . . . *48*
class R-67, 4-8-4 . . . *144, 184*
(gas electric), B-B . . . *247*
model F-T, B-B . . . *Jacket*
model TA, B-B . . . *204*
model E-6, A1A-A1A . . . *217*
model DL-109, A1A-A1A . . . *211*

Chicago, South Shore & South Bend

class (steeple cab), B-B . . . *280*
class ("Little Joe"), 4-D+D-4 . . . *282*

Colorado & Southern

class (Santa Fe), 2-10-2 . . . *50-51*

Delaware & Hudson

class J, 4-6-6-4 . . . *108-109*
model RS-3, B-B . . . *255, 256*
model Century-628, C-C . . . *250*

Delaware, Lackawanna & Western

class 101, 4-6-2 . . . *121*
class (Pocono), 4-8-4 . . . *120*

Denver & Rio Grande Western

class M-64, 4-8-4 . . . *49*
class M-68, 4-8-4 . . . *53*
class L-131, 2-8-8-2 . . . *53, 151*
class L-105, 4-6-6-4 . . . *150*

Denver & Rio Grande Western (N.G.)

class K-36, 2-8-2 . . . *192*
class K-37, 2-8-2 . . . *192*

Electro Motive Division

#103, model F-T, B-B . . . *206*
Demo model SD-45, C-C . . . *250*

Erie Railroad

class K-1, 4-6-2 . . . *116*
class K-5, 4-6-2 . . . *43*
class R-1, 2-10-2 . . . *123*
class S-2, 2-8-4 . . . *123*
class S-3, 2-8-4 . . . *116*
model F-A, B-B . . . *220*
model Pa, A1A-A1A . . . *232*

Erie-Lackawanna

model SW-7, B-B . . . *295*
model U34CH, C-C . . . *293*
model SD-45, C-C . . . *294*

Georgia Pacific

(Shay-Geared) . . . *285*

Great Northern Railway

class S-1, 4-8-4 . . . *158*
class M-2, 2-6-8-0 . . . *157*
class N-3, 2-8-8-0 . . . *157*
class R-2, 2-8-8-2 . . . *158*

Grand Trunk Western

class K-4-a, 4-6-2 . . . *24*
class U-4-b, 4-8-4 . . . *77*

Gulf, Mobile & Ohio

Rebel (non-articulated), B-B . . . *61*
model S-2, B-B . . . *221*
DL-109, A1A-A1A . . . *212, 221*
model F-3, B-B . . . *224-225*
model F-A, B-B . . . *221*
model SD-40, C-C . . . *292*

Illinois Central

class (Mikado), 2-8-2 . . . *194*
class (Mountain), 4-8-2 . . . *272*
model E-7, A1A-A1A . . . *203, 218*
model E-8, A1A-A1A *Jacket* . . . *195*

Kansas City Southern

class J, 2-10-4 . . . *140*

Lehigh & Hudson River

class (Consolidation), 2-8-0 . . . *118*
class (Mountain), 4-8-2 . . . *119*
model Century 420, B-B . . . *290*

Lehigh Valley

class K-5 *(John Wilkes)*, 4-6-2 . . . *79*
class T-1, 4-8-4 . . . *123*
model F-A, B-B . . . *220*
model PA, A1A-A1A . . . *232*

Louisville & Nashville

class M-1, 2-8-4 . . . *168*
model E-6, A1A-A1A . . . *207*

Magma Arizona Railroad

class (Consolidation), 2-8-0 . . . *286*

Maine Central

class S, 2-8-2 . . . *96*
class S1, 2-8-2 . . . *96, 99*
model GP-7, B-B . . . *254-255*

Maryland & Pennsylvania Railroad

class (Consolidation), 2-8-0 . . . *8*

Missouri Pacific Lines

class MK-63,
2-8-2 . . . *48, 138, 139, 148*
class MT-73, 4-8-2 . . . *139*
class MT-75, 4-8-2 . . . *214-215*
class SF-63, 2-10-2 . . . *46*
class NOR-75, 4-8-4 . . . *47*
model E-6, A1A-A1A . . . *216*
model E-7, A1A-A1A . . . *219*
model PA, A1A-A1A . . . *230-234*

Mobile & Gulf

class (Mogul), 2-6-0 . . . *285*

Monon Railroad

model BL-2, B-B . . . *255*
model F-7, B-B . . . *238*

Nashville, Chattanooga & St. Louis

class J-3, 4-8-4 . . . *89*

New York Central System

class H-10b, 2-8-2 . . . *Jacket*
class F-12a, 4-6-0 . . . *112-113*
class K-3, 4-6-2 . . . *111*
class K-3n, 4-6-2 . . . *136*
class K-5 *(James Whitcomb Riley),* 4-6-2 . . . *71*
class K-5 (Mercury) . . . *71*
class J-1a,
4-6-4 . . . *40, 170, 182, 183*
class J-3c ("Commodore Vanderbilt"), 4-6-4 . . . *64*
class J-3c (Dreyfuss),
4-6-4 . . . *72, 73, 74, 75, 78, 81*
class J-3a *(Empire State Express),* 4-6-4 . . . *80*
class Super J-3a, 4-6-4 . . . *110*
class L-2c, 4-8-2 . . . *32*
class L-3a, 4-8-2 . . . *12, 179*
class L-4b, 4-8-2 . . . *111, 181*
class S1-b, 4-8-4 . . . *95, 137, 178*
model F-A, B-B . . . *222*
model DR-4-4-15, B-B . . . *229*
model F-7, B-B . . . *240-241*
model DR -6-4-15 ("Babyface"),
A1A-A1A . . . *226*
model CFA-20-4 (C-Liner),
B-B . . . *243*
class P, 2-C+C-2 . . . *281*

New York, New Haven & Hartford

class Y-4, 0-8-0 . . . *107*
class L-1, 2-10-2 . . . *30, 107*
class I-4, 4-6-2 . . . *104, 106*
class I-5, 4-6-4 . . . *69*
class R-3, 4-8-2 . . . *106*
Comet (bi-directional),
diesel . . . *61*
model RS-3, B-B . . . *256*
model DL-109, A1A-A1A . . . *213*
model PA, A1A-A1A . . . *231*
class EP-3, 2-C+C-2 . . . *278*
class EP-5, C-C . . . *278*
class EF-4, C-C . . . *279*

New York, Ontario & Western

class Y-1, 4-8-2 . . . *33*
class Y-2, 4-8-2 . . . *117*

New York, Susquehanna & Western

class J-2, 2-10-0 . . . *117*

Nickel Plate Road

class L-1a, 4-6-4 . . . *193*
class S, 2-8-4 . . . *271*
class S-3, 2-8-4 . . . *270*
model PA, A1A-A1A . . . *235*

Norfolk & Western Railway

class K-2, 4-8-2 . . . *10, 169, 170*
class J, 4-8-4 . . . *80*
class A, 2-6-6-4 . . . *260*
class Y-6, 2-8-8-2 . . . *261, 262, 263*

Northern Pacific

class A-4, 4-8-4 . . . *154, 155*
class Z-3, 2-8-8-2 . . . *156*
class Z-6, 4-6-6-4 . . . *159*

Northwestern Steel & Wire

class (Consolidation), 2-8-0 . . . *1*

Oregon & Northwestern

class (Mikado), 2-8-2 . . . *159*

Pennsylvania Railroad

class K-4s,
4-6-2 . . . *40, 41, 134-135, 170*
class K-4s (Loewy), 4-6-2 . . . *59*
class K-4s (streamlined),
4-6-2 . . . *171*
class H-6, 2-8-0 . . . *170*
class L-1, 2-8-2 . . . *35*
class I-1sa, 2-10-0 . . . *264*

class J-1a, 2-10-4 . . . *265*
class M-1b, 4-8-2 . . . *34*
class S-1, 6-4-4-6 . . . *78-79*
class Q-2, 4-4-6-4 . . . *135*
class S-2, 6-8-6 . . . *134*
model DR-4-4-15, B-B . . . *229*
model DR -12-8-1500/2 ("Centipede"), 2-D+D-2 . . . *226*
model DR -6-4-20, A1A-A1A . . . *226*
model PA, A1A-A1A . . . *233*
class GG-1, 2-C+C-2 . . . *283*

Reading Company

class K-1sa, 2-10-2 . . . *122*

Richmond Fredericksburg & Potomac

class (Potomac), 4-8-4 . . . *11*

Seaboard

class P-2, 4-6-2 . . . *37*
class B-1, 2-10-2 . . . *36*

Soo Line

class 0-20, 4-8-4 . . . *184*

Southern Pacific Lines

class MT-4, 4-8-2 . . . *165*
class GS-4, 4-8-4 . . . *82, 84-85, 87*
class AC-7, 4-8-8-2 . . . *198*
class AC-11, 4-8-8-2 . . . *165*
class AC-12, 4-8-8-2 . . . *162*

Southern Railway

class Ks, 2-8-0 . . . *39*
class MS-4, 2-8-2 . . . *36*
class Ss, 2-10-2 . . . *28*
class Ls-2, 2-8-8-2 . . . *37*
class PS-4, 4-6-2 . . . *126*
class Ts-1, 4-8-2 . . . *38*
model E-8, A1A-A1A . . . *242*

Spokane, Portland & Seattle

class Z-6, 4-6-6-4 . . . *160*
model F-A, B-B . . . *288*
model GP-9, B-B . . . *288*
model Century 636, B-B . . . *289*

St. Johnsbury & Lamoille County

class K, 0-6-0 . . . *97*

St. Louis-Southwestern (Frisco)

class (Northern), 4-8-4 . . . *141*
model VO-1000, B-B . . . *219*
model F-A, B-B . . . *222*

Sydney & Louisburg

class (Consolidation), 2-8-0 . . . *199*

Texas & Pacific

class M-1, 4-8-2 . . . *90, 151*
class M-2, 4-8-2 . . . *150*

Toledo, Peoria & Western

class H-10, 4-8-4 . . . *91*

Twin Seams Coal Co.

(Shay-geared) . . . *287*

Union Pacfic

class (Pacific), 4-6-2 . . . *144*
class (MacArthur), 2-8-2 . . . *55, 161, 163, 196*
class (Mountain), 4-8-2 . . . *55*
class (Northern), 4-8-4 . . . *153, 164*
class (Santa Fe), 2-10-2 . . . *148*
class 4-10-2 . . . *164*
class (Union Pacific type), 4-12-2 . . . *Jacket 23, 52, 144, 145, 148, 149, 152*
class (Mallet), 2-8-8-0 . . . *224*
class (Challenger), 4-6-6-4 . . . *275*
class (Big Boy), 4-8-8-4 . . . *197, 274, 275*
model M-10000 (articulated), distillate . . . *58*
model M-10001 (articulated), diesel . . . *65*
#CD-07A, B, C, *(City of Denver)*, B-B . . . *65, 67*
#LA-1, 2, 3, class E-2 *(City of Los Angeles)*, A1A-A1A . . . *65*
model F-3, B-B . . . *224*
model PA, A1A-A1A . . . *233*
model GP-9, B-B . . . *257*
model U-50, B-B-B-B . . . *292*

Virginian Railway

class EL-C, C-C . . . *283*

Wabash Railroad
class P-1, 4-6-4 . . . *90*

Washington & Old Dominion
(gas-electric), B-B . . . *246*

Western Maryland Railway
class H-7b, 2-8-0 . . . *124*
class I-2, 2-10-0 . . . *125*
class M-2, 4-6-6-4 . . . *125*

Western Pacific
class MK-60, 2-8-2 . . . *161*
class M-137, 2-8-8-2 . . . *209*
model F-T, B-B . . . *209*
model F-7, B-B . . . *239*